Dr. JOHN TRENT - If you're perfect and have zero struggles in your life – then put down this book right now. But if you're like I am, and you've struggled with life, past hurts, and broken dreams and challenging relationships – AND if in the midst all that, you are ready to REALLY find freedom and life - then I believe you'll find as much help and encouragement as I did in reading this book. It has been my honor to know Carter Featherston personally for years. He has an incredible mind and intellect, but you won't find "hard to understand" concepts here. Just hard won wisdom and life-impacting insights that have changed Carter's life – and can turn around your life-story as well. So if you're ready to finally find that wisdom and REST you've been longing for – then read this book!

Trent, Ph.D.
nt, StrongFamilies.com
. Chapman Chair of Marriage and
Ministry and Therapy
Theological Seminary
Author of *The Blessing* and *LifeMapping*

CHUCK BENTLEY - "Carter Featherston has written about a topic he knows painfully well, recovery from shame. After resigning from the pastorate because of an addiction, he discovered a path to hope and restoration- a deep understanding of our true identity. This is an important work because so many suffer guilt and shame, especially over financial mistakes. Find your identity in Christ and be set free."

—Chuck Bentley
CEO, Crown Financial Ministries
Founder and Executive Director,
Christian Economic Forum
Author of four books, including
The Worst Financial Mistakes in the Bible;
and How You Can Avoid Them
and *THRIVE; How to Do Well in Any Economy*
He has written articles for major newspapers,
magazines, and speaks all around the world.

JOSH MCDOWELL - Carter Featherston has written with a fresh voice on the healing of the wounds of the past, and changing at the deepest level, the level of Identity. And he is someone who has done it. Resigning from the pastorate because of his own failure and brokenness, God met Carter in his story. Let him teach you how to meet God in your story, and let Him change you where it matters most, at the level of Identity.

> —Josh McDowell
> Author, Speaker, Evangelist to The Culture &
> Humanitarian
> Authored/Co-Authored over 145 Books
> *More Than A Carpenter* (27 million +)
> *Evidence That Demands a Verdict* (a top 40 Book
> in 20th Century)
> Four-time Gold Medallion Book Award Winner

Dr. KEN BOA - Carter Featherston's honest exposé of the struggles he encountered as a pastor with serious addictions is a clear portrayal of the redemptive power of God who transmutes pain into a life ministry. The hard-learned insights he gained through the process of wrestling with a shame-based identity and discovering an authentic grace-based identity are poignant and relevant to people who need to come out of hiding and discover their true stories in Christ.

> —Kenneth Boa, Author, Speaker, and President of
> Reflections Ministries
> He has authored/co-authored and served as editor
> for over a hundred books and study Bibles, and is
> a three-time Gold Medallion Book Award Winner

DR. TIM DINGER - "This book is a pastoral and passionate plea to embrace the love of God you've always wanted but thought you were disqualified to ever have. Gentle but persuasive, Carter shares from the depths of his experience to help you stop hiding and open yourself to the loving embrace of God."

> —Dr. Tim Dinger is the Associate Dean and
> director of the Student Counseling Center,

and an adjunct professor in the Graduate
Counseling Program,
John Brown University, Siloam Springs, AR

RICHARD EXLEY - "I am a voracious reader but it is not often I pick up a book that speaks to me in the way "God Knows Your Story and He's Not Mad" did. Carter Featherston's writing is captivating and his message is point on!"

> —Richard Exley, Pastor and Denominational Leader
> Author of several books such as *Man of Valor* and
> *The Making of a Man*
> His articles have appeared in numerous magazines
> including *Leadership Journal, Charisma, Ministries
> Today, Advance, Enrichment* and *New Man*

MAX DAVIS - "God has used Carter Featherston in my own life in a deeply profound way. As a Christian I was locked in a prison of performance, thinking God was angry at me, and that He only loved me if I behaved well. Shame followed me wherever I went, and affected my relationships and my marriage. Carter has helped me come to understand that God knows my story . . . every ugly detail, and He's still in love with me! Meeting God in my story changed my life. This book will teach you how to dialogue with God about your own story. I'm sure it will set you free, too."

> —Max Davis has written over 30 books published
> with such notable publishers as Worthy,
> Zondervan, Thomas Nelson, and Destiny Image
> Bantam Doubleday Dell, Cook, Penguin Putnam.
> He is the author of *When Jesus was a Green-Eyed
> Brunette*; and his bestseller, *Insanity of Unbelief; a
> Journalist's Journey from Belief, to Skepticism, to
> Deep Faith.*
> His books have been translated into several
> languages and have been featured on
> The Today Show, USA Today, Publisher's Weekly,
> and The 700 Club.

God Knows Your Story . . .
(and He's Not Mad!)

THE CONVERSATION HE WANTS.
THE TRANSFORMATION YOU WANT.

by
CARTER FEATHERSTON

God Knows Your Story . . . and He's Not Mad!
The Conversation He Wants. The Transformation You Want.
ISBN: 978-1-939570-85-7
Copyright © 2018 by Carter Featherston

Published by Word and Spirit Publishing
P.O. Box 701403
Tulsa, Oklahoma 74170
wordandspiritpublishing.com

DEDICATION

This book is dedicated to everyone I have hurt.

"For your goodness and love pursue me all the days of my life."

(Psalm 23:6 in The Passion Translation)

CONTENTS

ACKNOWLEDGMENTS

I want to thank my wife, Cindy, for enduring the journey our marriage has been. Without you I would not have written this book, and we wouldn't have the ministry that we have today. Thank you for listening to God and trusting Him for our marriage. Many of our friends today honor you, too, for your strong faith in the Father.

I want to thank my Board of Directors (Ern & Cindy Carrier, Kathy Cooke, Perry & Julianna Dougherty, Onalise Malik and Jeff & Edie Mitchell), for your encouragement and support for these many years. You have made me more mature, and have covered me after many mistakes. I am amazed at how a band of wonderful people could be so committed to a man like me. You have kept me focused on loving the Body of Christ, and honoring Him with my words.

Thanks, too, goes to my dear friend and author, Max Davis. Max sharpens me. He critiques my writing —-even tells me when my writing is boring! Our friendship is a great joy to me. (If you like the title of this book, Max came up with it after we spent two days brainstorming. Early on the third day, he arose and texted me, "I've got it . . . here's the title!" That's how good he is.) Thank you, my friend.

As well, I would like to thank three couples for their support in getting this project across the goal line: Daniel and Karen Bonvillain, Ty and Shawna Gose, and Curtis and Christie Jack. Thank you for being examples of those who have lived the truths I write about in this book, and have worked on your own hearts to have marriages that glorify God. I'm glad to be a part of your journeys.

Thank you, Keith Provance, and your team at Word & Spirit Publishing. I'm so grateful for your enthusiasm over this book, and your guidance in getting it done. I couldn't be more pleased.

DIALOGUE:

God's Plan for Transformation

CHAPTER 1

Our Stories Begin with Hiding

I grew up skinny and slow. Yep, a very discouraging combination. Discouraging that is, if you wanted to compete in sports around the neighborhood. If you wanted to invent computers, as a couple of boys from my generation grew up to do, then skinny and slow wouldn't hurt too much. But before the age of cell phones and computers, when kids lived and played outdoors, it was a distinct disadvantage.

I wasn't very strong, either, but early in grade school my friends and I accepted each other. I was an average kid, feeling mostly adequate and self-secure, and life was pretty good. We rode bikes and played alongside the irrigation ditch, where the first rite of passage in our neighborhood was to be brave enough to keep your balance on a twelve-inch pipe and cross over the irrigation ditch without falling in the water. We built forts in fields, in backyards, and even up in trees. We shot our BB guns and fished. We played football in the Yancey backyard and baseball in the big open field next door. All was well, through the fourth grade.

For me, life changed forever in the fifth grade. For boys, there comes a day around that age when life takes on a competitive edge; when fierceness, toughness, and the ability to intimidate another boy become merit badges in the quest for masculine superiority. Winners take all, losers go home. The strong guys talk tough, and the weaker ones keep quiet. Winners know who they are, and losers had better know their boundaries and stay in line. It's around the fifth grade that every boy, either quietly or boisterously, initiates his journey into image management.

In the fifth grade I became acquainted with the driving force we know today as Shame. At age eleven, skinny and slow now mattered. Significantly. The pecking order now mattered. Regrettably. For these things determined who was captain in choosing up sides, who played and who sat out, who got attention from the girls or who got ignored. Winners won. Losers found strategies to juke and jive, laugh and survive, as shame quietly took up residence in the heart.

On the inside, despair began to emerge. I didn't like *who* I was. I didn't like *how* I was. I was a Christian kid, growing more and more ashamed of how God made me. And when I hit puberty, a whole new fight broke out, and it seemed the gates of Hell were prevailing!

Most men I talk to today acknowledge the same fight. In high school we found it hard to reconcile our sexual life with walking with God. Guilt, secrecy, and a shameful identity became the themes of our life. By the end of high school many of us had given up on living for God. We felt like failures as some of us checked out spiritually.

By the end of high school my identity was built around my sense of inadequacy, my shame, and my secrets. Living a defeated life, my story was filled with:

Pain.

Anger.

Hurtful memories.

Fear.

Shame.

All this with church on Sundays . . . and even Sunday nights!

I was defeated in my desire to please God and hoped that I could change—that I could turn things around. You know—be more disciplined, be stronger. Instead I felt like a misfit. Still juking and jiving, laughing and surviving—I felt like a failure, and I was covering up the shame.

So . . . what did I do?

I went off to Bible college!

I went there primarily for one reason, so that I could play basketball. I had made the team the last two years of high school, as basketball became a way to hide my feelings of inadequacy. For where else could a skinny kid build a decent reputation, but by out-jumping and out-scoring his peers on the court? I wasn't too bad, either—not too bad for a skinny kid.

When I got to Bible college, I found a new way to hide. Education became my new fig leaf, to cover up the pain of my shameful story of defeat. Posturing as a Biblical Apologetics Know-It-All gave me the appearance of having it all together.

And it worked . . . *for a while.*

I was popular and funny, and I was even granted positions of leadership, but deep down in my gut I knew the truth. I was a fraud, but wouldn't face it. I was self-deceived, and I was missing the internal peace that integrity brings.

Like Adam, we try to hide what we think is a secret. But God knows, and He knows that it blocks our intimacy with Him. Adam was stuck—hiding and thinking fig leaves would cover his shame.

We, too, are stuck, hiding and thinking a false self will cover our shame.

I was once in a "Men's Accountability Group," where subconsciously I wasn't planning to be the least bit accountable. I was planning on hiding. In fact, faithfully showing up every week was part of my scam! If I showed up, then you thought I was fully engaged. But I wasn't. I was hiding.

And I was the pastor.

So, if a pastor is hiding, then what's going on in the pews? Apparently, I helped build our national institution of hiding behind *image management* and *false identities.* We printed in the Sunday bulletin that we were "*doing life together,*" but in my own life and in my observations as a minister, it's more like we were *avoiding* life together. We avoided the true stories of our pain, anger, shame, and secrets. We hid behind the masks of our false selves. We're not supposed to talk about that pain . . . are we? "Forget what lies behind and press on" . . . right?

Missing the Crux?

I have a well-educated guess as to why we are not doing meaningful discipleship today. From conversations with leaders, and observations in churches, I think it's because the people we disciple—especially the men—almost never make lasting and meaningful changes in their lives. We've all seen this. We are teaching the right doctrine, how to have better families, and how to put our finances in biblical order! But that's all we are doing—teaching.

We are teaching, but we are not transforming.

We are neglecting the *interior condition* of our disciples. We have completely ignored their interior strongholds and the backstory that created them.

We need to help people with their backstories of pain and shame, but there was no class for this in seminary. So, we don't know how. I never got any help with my heart in the early days of my education and ministry. The Bible training and spiritual life classes in my Christian experience were not helping me with my backstory. I had plenty of study on theology and apologetics, but I completely ignored the conflicts in my heart.

Many of us pastors have tried various programs and venues, but nothing has worked very well. In my experience, very few lives have change beyond a few weeks of emotional excitement, so we have quietly given up. The thought of one more program makes the men of our churches run away. As a pastor I talked and talked, but hardly ever listened. I was not able to help others with the backstories of their wounded hearts. I mean, good grief, I wasn't even working on mine!

And here's one more concern. Our most popular books today seem to be devotionals! Oh, it's a fine thing, I suppose, to read a page in your devotional booklet, and then pray the prayer at the bottom. But do you realize that you are reading about someone else's experience with God? If that's all you do, how will you ever mature?[1]

In fact, it appears today that we have to send people to a Christian counselor so that they can finally do the discipleship work of getting delivered from their backstory—for $125 an hour!

---

[1] I certainly believe that *My Utmost for His Highest* (Chambers) and *Jesus Calling* (Young) should be on everyone's shelf. And a devotional book can be encouraging to a new believer, or comforting in a challenging season of life. But the Christian life cannot be nourished into maturity solely on the reading of devotionals.

Something's wrong! This needs to change. For most of our spiritual training is leaving this transformational work on the interior condition, at the least, unfinished, and at the worst, untouched!

All great spiritual discoveries and breakthroughs come from a deep inner journey, a journey rooted in dialogue. I found my deepest transformation through dialogue with God. I want to help you find yours.

God wants to have a conversation with you.

At the cross God set you free from the penalty of your sins, but in dialogue He sets you free from the *persecution* of your sins.

The sins of your story condemn you.

The secrets of your story shame you.

They knock you down and deflate you.

Your story can have more control over your life than God does!

He wants to set you free, but He can't free what you won't see.

Wherever you are in life, whatever has happened in your past, it doesn't matter how dark or how low, how much you've failed, or even how much you've succeeded! God wants to have a dialogue with you. He's already initiated the conversation. It's in authentic dialogue with our Redeemer that transformation comes, and we are released from defeat and discouragement, from bondage and brokenness, and even from our own self-deceptions.

Our healing comes in looking up, in prayerfully doing our healing work. God wants to dialogue with you. Not to bring up your past to condemn you, but to free you from your past to transform you.

This book is not about how I prayed the Jabez prayer and God blessed me, so my family is fantastic and my ministry is terrific! No.

My qualifications to write this book are twofold: I have *outrageously failed* in life as my story finally defeated me; but I cried out to God, Who answered me and showed me great and hidden things I did not know (Jeremiah 33:3). This book is about what I learned on that journey.

CHAPTER 2

What's in Your Story?

"Nothing makes a man so lonely as his secrets."

—Paul Tournier

I was a man with secrets. We all have them, and secrets can be very condemning. Secrets give birth to shame, and shame is not a mere emotion. It is an identity built around your lack of ability to accept yourself and be comfortable in your own skin. It's the fear that you will somehow be "revealed and seen" for who you are, and then no one will accept you. Secrets make us afraid, giving birth to shame, and shame moves us to feel unworthy in the sight of God.

Yes, we "know" God supposedly forgives us. We are forgiven for everything, even if it's done in secret. It's all forgiven. I knew this was true. I'd heard it a hundred times in Sunday School, and was now even teaching it to others, yet I struggled to believe it for myself. I might be forgiven, but surely He's mad. *I'm a failure; I'm despicable; and I'm a complete disappointment to God!* That's what I really believed about myself. So, for many years, I shrank back, discouraged and ashamed, promoting myself in ministry, but hiding my heart from public view.

Hidden to others, even hiding from myself, I wasn't hiding anything from God. It wasn't until years later, when He and I entered into an honest dialogue, that freedom came. When God enters our stories, He can change us at the place where it matters the most, at the level of Identity. He can heal us from our shame-based identity, and establish us in our grace-based identity, in Christ. He can remove the haunting of the pain and anger, the frustration and fear. He can heal us from the hurtful memories that play over and over in our minds. God can cancel out the power of a wounded identity and open our eyes to see our new identity in Him.

Stuck in the Secrets

Adam was stuck in the secrets of his life.

"Adam, where are you?"

In other words, *"Adam, what's the story now? What's happened? Why are you hiding? Are you stuck? Who told you that? Who lied to you? Who hurt you? Who wounded you? Where's it broken? What are you afraid of? Who do you think you're fooling? Are you still blaming others?"*

God's dialogue with Adam was to expose his secret and set him free, to open his eyes to see where freedom lay. Isn't this similar to what Jesus announced that He was here to do? The ministry of Jesus began that day when He stood up before his local congregation and read from Isaiah 61. He announced that He was now present and available to set captives free, to cause spiritually and physically blind people to see, and to bring freedom to those who are bound up . . . like, say, people who are hiding.

So, what about your past? What keeps you hiding? What keeps you from walking in freedom? Are you discouraged? Ashamed? Angry at someone? Angry at yourself? Do you doubt that you're wanted? That you are deserving? Do you doubt God's love for you? Think He's disappointed with you? Disappointed with Him?

Today, God uses me to help others find healing and freedom from the painful issues in their lives. On the retreats I now lead, called Pure Heart Weekend, I meet others just like I was: people whose stories so control them that they are unable to live in the freedom that Christ bought them. I even get men to tell me their stories! I meet with wonderful people who are sincere Christians, but who are defeated and frustrated because of their stories:

- ◆ Stories of a parent's rage, with slaps, pulls, yanks, and beatings.
- ◆ Stories of violence, trauma, and abuse of every kind.
- ◆ Stories of lonely tears from abandonment; orphans in their own homes.
- ◆ Stories of addictions, sadness, and pain.
- ◆ Stories of divorces, and the tearing apart.
- ◆ Stories of school day humiliations and fears.

- ◆ Stories of violations, betrayal, and rejection.
- ◆ Stories of broken hearts and lovers that ran away.
- ◆ Stories that led to secret sins.

Out of these stories emerge broken identities. As believers we may appear all together on the outside, but on the inside we battle with identities like, *I'm Unworthy, I'm Unwanted, I'm a Reject, I'm Unforgiven; I'm Still Pending Approval*—thus, I don't deserve to be blessed by God.

These broken identities come from wounded hearts; hearts full of judgments and complaints; hearts of bitterness and rage; of cowardice and weakness; hearts of stone and hearts of shame. When our hearts are full of these toxic attitudes, they can make us feel like a fraud.

We are Bible-reading and born again, yet so many of us find ourselves frustrated and defeated! We sit in church and wonder, *"How do you change all of this? Where do you get help for this?"* One pastor recognized this and exclaimed, "There's a crisis in our churches. Our people are not being dynamically transformed!"

That's right. Our story won't let us be.

Our story shames us; the story of what happened to us; how we began to think about it; and how we began to cope . . . with secret sins.

What's in your story?

CHAPTER 3

The Story at the Well

"Sometimes it lasts in love, but sometimes it hurts instead."

—Adele

Some of us are like Adam, hiding what he thought was a secret. Others of us are like the woman that Jesus met in John 4. Her secrets were out and known to the public, and they were causing her to hide. You remember the Woman at the Well? Now, she had a story!

It was the hottest part of the day—the lunch hour—when she showed up to draw water. She had come to the well alone. Why was she alone?

I'll tell you why. She was hiding.

Traditionally, the women of a town looked forward to being together in the morning as they went to the well to draw water. It was a social time to visit and swap stories. In some cases, they traveled together for safety's sake, and especially to this well—it was a half-mile out of town!

More importantly, it was typical for women to come in the cool of the morning to get their water for the needs of the day. So, why is she arriving in the early afternoon? Because she had secrets—which give birth to shame, and shame is what makes us hide. She was not welcome to be with other women. She had, like I said, a backstory.

It was hot . . . she was alone . . . and she was hiding.

What's in your story? Are you hiding from yourself and avoiding your heart? Are you hiding from others? Are you trying to hide from God?

This woman may have been fooling others and fooling herself, but she wasn't fooling Jesus. He knew that she needed more than a pitcher full of water. She needed the gift of God: His forgiveness and acceptance, and the release of her shame.

So, what did Jesus do? He initiated a dialogue with a simple question.

"Will you draw me a drink of water?"

She replied, "How is it that you, being a Jew, would ask me, a Samaritan, for a drink of water?" She knew the prejudices of the religious systems of the day, for the Jews regarded the Samaritans as an unclean people, and a conscientious Jew would not want to drink from the "defiled" water vessel of a Samaritan.

She knew what He might be thinking for she was already thinking it, too! She wore her shame on her sleeve, and gave herself away with her words. She so quickly revealed her neediness that He went straight to the sermon:

"If you knew the gift of God, and who I am, you would ask for a drink of water from Me, and I would give you living water."

He turned from His talk of mere drinking water and swerved into a discussion of the symbolism of water in the ancient writings of the prophets. "Living water" in the Old Testament was the symbol for the flowing water of cleansing and blessing, where even Yahweh Himself is called a fountain of living water (Jeremiah 2:13).

He followed with the application point: *"Whoever drinks of the water that I give will never be thirsty again."*

"Sir," the woman said, "give me this water."

She was thirsty, all right! Navigating through life the way she did, watching her steps and avoiding people. She had to be thirsty for meaningful relationships and parched for love and acceptance. Did she know that he wasn't talking about the water from a well? Did she have a sense that He was talking about quenching a spiritual thirst? Was it the love in His face? The peace in His eyes? Did she know that Jesus was talking about quenching the thirst of a dry and empty heart?

Something was stirring inside her, and she was ready to receive His offer, but then He does something the woman doesn't expect. Just when she thought, *Oh good, I can hide my story and still get in on this amazing water offer,* Jesus stuns her. He turns the dialogue to expose her story. She had to see her need for the offer to mean anything, so before He invited her to walk the aisle, Jesus exposed her present sleeping arrangement.

"First, go get your husband, and come back here together."

You've got to be kidding, she must have thought. *How did He know?*

But He did know. The Father "shows" Jesus what He needs to "see,"[2] so Jesus knew that this woman standing before Him was the product of painful marital and sexual brokenness.

She confessed her story, "I have no husband."

"You are right in saying that you have no husband, for you have had five, and the one you now live with is not your husband. Isn't that true?"

He knew her story!

Jesus knew what was inside of her all along. He knows what's inside of you. You may think you're hiding your story from God, but you're not hiding. He knows, and He's not mad. He wants to quench your thirst. He knows your story, so He must know the broken places of your heart. If He's counted the number of hairs on your head, then how much more does He know the wounds in your heart?

This woman needed healing in her heart from five rejections and divorces, and the public shame that must have

---

[2] John 5:19,30.

surrounded her every day as she went to the public market and shopped in the presence of the other women. It's more than likely that she was an adulteress, too, unfaithful in her marriages, thus warranting that all five husbands would "put her away."

Today, we know well that adultery doesn't come out of left field in someone's life. Adultery is usually driven by a backstory. Perhaps early on she was sexually broken. She could've been molested as a young girl. Perhaps she had been promiscuous before her first marriage. For those who are sexually wounded, sex is often used selfishly to achieve a false sense of love and acceptance. So it's not hard at all to imagine that this woman at the well was a five-time divorcee because of the story of her emotional, relational, and sexual baggage. She would have been desperate for "living water," desperate for the love and acceptance of Father God.

But amazingly, she was still determined to hide her story! She turns the conversation to religion and asks which church . . . er, I mean . . . which mountain (the Jew's mountain or the Samaritan's mountain) was the right one for true worship. But she was blowing smoke. Jesus turned her distraction right back on the target—her need. *"The day has come, now, where it does not matter about mountains or cities for worshiping God. For true worshipers are those who worship God in spirit and in truth."*

Bingo! *In truth.*

Ah-ha!

Yes, God's truth will set you free . . . *especially the truth about yourself!*

Freedom comes not in merely getting saved and going to church. Freedom comes when God plainly reveals to you where you are stuck and trapped in the prison of your own pain and cover-up, like this woman. Like Adam.

Doesn't He still do that?

Freedom comes in our lives when we present ourselves to Him in all the honesty and transparency (the truth!) of our back-stories: our traumas, our scandals, others' sins against us, and the lies we've bought. He leads us in the spiritual work of receiving His comfort, breaking bondages, renouncing lies, opening our eyes to see the real truth and setting us free from our self-judgments and condemnation. Jesus pursues us in our stories to set us free from our past, and He pursued this woman at the well to get her to tell her story. Then she could see her need for His love and acceptance and allow it to heal her heart.

He got her to tell her story.

Not because He was mad at her!

Not to condemn her, nor judge her, nor add to her shame.

He did it to draw her into dialogue . . . loving and safe; to get her to tell the story from which she needed healing and redemption. When she could own the truth of her pain and shame, then she could exchange it for His healing love and grace.

Spiritual transformation is rooted in dialogue. All great spiritual discoveries are rooted in dialogue. Jesus got the conversation that He wanted. The woman got the transformation that she needed. This is how Freedom emerges in our lives.

Our God is dialogical . . . and He wants a conversation with you.

CHAPTER 4

Why Is God Always Asking Questions?

"I will take my stand at my watch post . . . and look out to see what God will say to me."

—Habakkuk 2:1

Brenda called to set an appointment with me. She and her husband were having a problem. She claimed it was his history with pornography. When they arrived and took a seat, Brenda was more in control, as Phil looked down, nervous and quiet. He picked at the lint on his pants.

We started into the session and they began to describe what was going on in their home and with their intimacy. Yes, Phil did have a history with porn, as so many husbands do. But that was not their only problem.

After a few more sessions, meeting separately with each of them, it became apparent that Brenda had a huge problem, too, perhaps every bit as big as Phil's problem. She had a problem with a crippling insecurity and deep identity of unworthiness. Her problem came out of her as a scathing, attacking, demanding, fighting-against-her-husband problem! Because of her own childhood rejections, Brenda felt inferior to the "woman" of Phil's pornographic mind. His sexual absence from their relationship triggered a deep sense of unworthiness that came out of her in a frightening way.

The story of Brenda's family of origin was one of chaos and hurt. Often as a child she was made to feel inferior, unattractive, and unworthy. It was compounded devastatingly in junior high school when she was rejected—verbally for all to hear—by the boys because of her looks.

Now, we definitely worked on Phil's problem, but to heal their marriage I had to gently call Brenda into dialogue. I had to get her to talk about her own heart, about the story that accompanied her into the marriage. Though legitimate hurt and anger were appropriate in light of Phil's problem, there was something extra intense about her anger. When she opened up to my questions, we discovered the ultimate source of her unhappiness. Her deepest pain was from avoiding her own story, and not entering into dialogue with God about her own shame. She was avoiding the healing that she, too, needed.

To get emotionally and spiritually healthy, just like Phil and Brenda, each one of us must acknowledge our need for a healing dialogue with God about the painful story behind our shame. We cannot change or heal what we do not acknowledge, and acknowledgement initiates a dialogue.

Our healing begins in recognizing a lost principle about what it means to be made in the image of God. The theology of being created in the image of God is a doctrinal point that has produced volumes of brilliant, insightful, and inspiring theology. You could read for years if you are interested in that. However, I would like to draw your attention to one of the least developed ideas in the textbooks: *To be made in the image of God is to be dialogical.*

To be *dialogical* means that we are a questioning, reasoning, evaluating, discerning person of *dialogue*. How do I know this? Chapter and verse? I see it in many scriptural passages. For when God shows up to engage human beings, He is often asking questions. He had four questions for Adam and Eve in Genesis 3:

> *"Adam, where are you?*
> *Who told you that you were naked?*
> *Have you eaten of the tree?*
> *What is this that you have done?"*

Next, in chapter 4:

> *"Cain, why are you so angry?*
> *Where is Abel, your brother?*
> *What have you done?"*

God had questions for Jacob, Jonah, Job, and Jeremiah. He asked questions of Moses and Elijah, as well as Isaiah and Ezekiel. Even Balaam and Satan got one question apiece.

In the Gospels, Jesus was asking questions, too. The Sermon on the Mount alone includes about fifteen. In one-on-one conversations with individuals, Jesus asked some questions that have since become famous.

"What does it profit a man if he gains the whole world, yet forfeits his own soul?"

"Do you want to get well?"

"Oh, you of little faith; why are you so afraid?"

Most famously, He asked Peter three times, *"Do you love Me?"*

If the Father and the Son are always asking questions, do we need to wonder what the Holy Spirit is doing as He indwells us? If the Holy Spirit is supposed to lead us into all truth (John 14:17; 1 John 2:27), will He not need to engage us with questions?

Father, Son, and Holy Spirit desire a walking, talking, dialoguing relationship with us, and that includes asking us questions. Why would God be asking us questions, unless we are dialogical? He created us for dialogue, *and He wants us to respond to Him.*

That's why Genesis 4:16 may be the saddest verse in the whole Bible, where it says Cain "departed from the presence of the Lord." The Hebrew word for "presence" is one of those powerfully descriptive words. The word is built around the word, "face." It is literally translated, "Cain turned and departed from in front of the face of God."

He walked out on dialogue.

He walked out on his opportunity for spiritual health.

He walked out on his moment for forgiveness, acceptance, and healing.

He turned and missed it all.

Why So Many Questions?

The purpose of a question is to start a dialogue. The purpose of dialogue is to lead us to self-awareness. The purpose of self-awareness is to initiate a transformation!

God's questions focus on our interior condition. He wants us to "see" what He has to "say" about what's going on inside our hearts. Spiritual, mental, and emotional growth is impossible without the *self-awareness* that comes through dialogue. It's how we come to learn about ourselves.

We can see *where* we are stuck. We can learn *why* we are stuck. We can discover *how* to get unstuck!

I can remember so many days in my addiction years where I purposefully avoided dialogue with God, just like Adam in the Garden and the Woman at the Well. I hid behind busyness and kept myself on the run . . . teaching somewhere, meeting somewhere, calling someone, eating somewhere, driving somewhere . . . and always listening to talk radio!

Noise. Distraction. Ministry. I never gave myself a chance to sit still and listen to God. I was afraid of dialogue. I think I was afraid of what I was going to hear.

Dialogue facilitates the opportunity for God to reveal to us the hurtful convictions and conclusions we have drawn from our pain, anger, hurtful memories, fear, and shame. These convictions and conclusions have us stuck in our spiritual growth, and dialogue is God's way of exposing this "unfinished business." By it we can be healed of our backstory, healed of our shame, and grow in our intimacy through our agreement with Him. Since God already knows us, He already knows the answers to His own questions, too, but He invites us into a dialogue so *we* can learn what it is that He already knows.

A Transparent Conversation of Honesty with God

The word *honesty* is from the Latin, "to own," as in *to own up to it; with no deceit or fraud; straightforward and pure.* We must learn to dialogue with God about our lack of honesty; that our wounds and brokenness have led to duplicity, deceitfulness, and dishonesty in our souls.

In dialogue we become persons, for a person is a human who is in relationship. In relationship with God we dialogue with Him about our hurts and our needs. *Who hurt us? What happened? What did they say?* We dialogue about our pride and our stubbornness. *At whom are we mad? Who will we not forgive? With whom are we embittered?* We dialogue about our selfishness and our reluctance to obey. *Why am I mad? Why am I a victim? Why do I deserve my selfish pleasures?* We can also fire questions right back at Him.

God meets us in our dialogue, and He changes our hearts through His questions. Perhaps this is what it originally meant for Christians to say that we have *a personal relationship with God*, i.e., we have a walking, talking, and dialoguing intimacy with Him.

So many Christians will not go back to talk honestly about their hurtful journey. I've talked with faithful, church-attending Christian men. *Angry, defensive, lecturing, always right, finger-in-your-face* Christian men who tell me that they don't have any wounds! They don't have anything like that to go back and pray about with Jesus. That's sad. Everyone in the room can see that these are wounded and unhealed men.

I've talked with praying, worshiping, hand-raising Christian women. *Emasculating, lecturing, defensive, closed-hearted, broken and hardened* Christian women who tell me that they don't have any wounds, either! They don't have anything that needs healing? Sad.

In dialogue with God we get healed. When we have no dialogue, we are left in our own monologue, and the self-talk of monologue is empty and futile. It actually causes the heart to grow darker and sicker. The consequences of monologue are recorded in one of the Apostle Paul's most hideous lists of the sins of humanity. It's all in Romans, chapter 1. Let's now consider what God says happens to us when we suppress the dialogue that He initiates.

CHAPTER 5

When Dialogue Stops, A Painful Penalty

For when I kept silent, my bones wasted away through my groaning all day long.

—Psalm 32:3

I taught a Bible class at church one Sunday morning, as a guest-substitute for the regular teacher. Keep in mind that I didn't know these folks very well. As I spoke on the themes of this book, an elegant woman, about seventy years old, spoke up. She was immaculately dressed and made-up. Her hair was magnificent, too. Her style told me that from her teens, she always has been a beautiful lady. Here was her question: "I seem to have seasons of my life where a depression comes upon me for three or four days in a row; it seems to come out of nowhere, and I just seem lost and separated from God . . . then, in a few days, it all goes away." She added, "Do you know what that is . . . what the problem might be?"

Now, I remind you, I didn't know these people very well. But this may be her only chance to hear this, so I decided not to chicken out. I looked at her kindly and said with great gentleness, "You have an old wound that you and God have never healed, and a couple of times a year something triggers that pain. It rises up to haunt you and shame you, sending you for several days into a depression of unworthiness before the Lord."

Tears came to her eyes. The room was quiet. I then added, "You and your husband should come meet with me at my office sometime soon. We can heal this."

I never heard from them.

Such blunt conversations are not often heard in Sunday School class; therefore, we feel awkward in their presence. We sit in silence, for we don't know how to respond. We are so new at learning about healing old wounds, triggers for depression, or healing the shame that binds us. So, we awkwardly move on and leave the class at the end of the hour, untouched by the close encounter we just had with the Way, the Truth, and the Life.

In the book of Romans, we see what can happen when we don't have dialogue with God. The first chapter tells the story of a people who rejected dialogue with God, and it put them in a terrible mess, inside and out.

In Romans 1:17-18, Paul says that the Gospel gives mankind two revelations. First, the presentation of the Gospel reveals that God is righteous—that's why there was a need for a payment for sin. The second revelation is that

God's wrath came against our sins when the payment was made. The preaching of the Gospel reveals the wrath of God, His wrath against the ungodliness and unrighteousness of men (John 3:36; Romans 5:9; Ephesians 2:3, 5:6).

But notice verse 18 of this passage. What do some people do with these revelations? They hold them down; they suppress them. They ignore the truth, and continue to live in their unrighteousness.

Note well: these people *did* receive the revelation. God initiated a conversation. He invited them into a dialogue. They received His revelation, but they ignored it. They suppressed His revelation and rejected the opportunity for a transforming conversation.

Now notice what happens when they continue to avoid dialogue. Verse 21 says, *"For although they knew God, they did not honor Him as God or give thanks to Him, but they became futile in their thinking, and their foolish hearts were darkened,"* (Romans 1:21).

Notice the first negative consequence when we suppress the dialogue that God has started: our worship and gratefulness die. We no longer have a heart for honor or thankfulness toward God.

Second, when the dialogue with God dies, then our own inner-talk is unhelpful to us. Different Bible translations say, "their speculations became futile" (NASB); "their thinking became futile" (NIV, ESV); "their imaginations became vain/useless" (KJV).

The Greek word for "speculations," "thinking," or "imaginations" is the word, *dialogismos*. Dialogue.

By suppressing God's revelation these people shut down the dialogue that He initiated, and their own *dialogismos* became futile, empty, and useless. Their self-dialogue could no longer help them. Today, this self-dialogue is what we call monologue. Spiritual growth and transformation can no longer happen in this condition of suppressing of the truth.

Third, with empty dialogue (monologue) there is no light from God in their hearts, and their thinking, decisions, and reasoning are "darkened." God is light, but if He is not in our thought-processes, then our thoughts are dark indeed.

When any person, believer or unbeliever, suppresses the truth, he or she is rejecting the revelation from God, and the dialogue stops. Mankind was created to be upright in dialogue with God. However, with no outside input from God, man's inward reasoning becomes useless and his heart gets darker.

Dark and Empty Monologue

Now, notice what happens. In the next two verses (Romans 1:22-23), as man is claiming to be so wise, he demonstrates his foolishness by worshipping creation, exchanging the worship of God for the worship of idols. Man is no longer upright in dialogue with God. Instead, man is *bent over in monologue*. He is bent over toward the earth, worshiping creation instead of the Creator.

Next comes the devastating consequence, in verse 24: *"Therefore, while living in the lusts of their hearts, God gave them over to impurity. . . ."* Notice what God *gave them over to*. He gave them over to *uncleanness*, or *impurity*. He did not give them over to lustful hearts—no, they already had that. God gave them over to *uncleanness* or *impurity*, and this is the Greek word, *akatharsis*.

Akatharsis is a word that refers to emotional cleansing. It is a word that speaks of the cleansing of our hearts. James calls it the "purifying of the heart" (James 4:8). Other ancient writers used this word to refer to the purging of negative emotions, or the purging of pent-up emotions so as to alleviate the tension and internal conflict. It is a word that refers to the cleansing of the heart from such things as grief, greed, envy, jealousy, bitterness, lust, or other negative emotions (and the thoughts behind them). In the English language we still speak of this cleansing, purifying action, but we spell it with a "c." We call it *catharsis*.

But wait! Notice the first letter of this Greek word, *akatharsis*. It's an *alpha (a)*. In the Greek when you want to negate a word, i.e., when you want to say "*not* this," then you put an *alpha* in the front. Therefore, this word is the opposite of *katharsis*. It's the word for "No-Catharsis." God gave these people over to a condition of having no cleansing of their painful emotions. They lived in a condition in which they *could not* purge their negative emotions, for they were in a monologue.

In a monologue you cannot cleanse your heart. You are left in a state of impurity and uncleanness of the heart.

Without catharsis, we get stuck in our negative emotions and internal conflicts that arise from painful events in our lives. We are stuck in emotional states of unforgiveness, bitterness, resentment, anger, sadness, regret, humiliation, or shame. We call this living with "unfinished business." All of these toxic states come from painful memories that we carry around in our hearts, because we have not healed them. We cleanse these negative emotions out of our hearts through healing dialogue with God. It is in prayerful dialogue with Him that we experience cleansing. Without catharsis we are unable to get healthy. We are unable to become mentally, emotionally, and spiritually healed.

So, get out of monologue and into dialogue. Self-talk is unclean and negative. It is rooted in our pain and hurt. In a monologue, we lose a heart for worship. We lose a heart of gratefulness. Our heart gets darker, sicker, and more unhealthy. The more we talk to ourselves without the light of God entering our hearts, the more emotionally, mentally, and spiritually unhealthy we become.

To summarize, these people in Romans 1 who suppressed the truth and rejected God's revelation ceased to be in dialogue with Him. They went from being upright in dialogue with God to being bent over in monologue with themselves. When we are bent over in monologue, we are unable to process the "unfinished business" of life, for example, the hurtful memories that result in unforgiveness and bitterness, sorrow and grief.

You cannot experience cathartic cleansing when you are in a monologue, for your thinking and reasoning will get sicker and darker. You will become stuck. You cannot purify your heart. You cannot get well. Without dialogue, you are in *akatharsis*, stuck in monologue, and unable to get spiritually cleansed from what is hurting your heart.

Now look at Roman 1:26-27. The result of *akatharsis* is sexual brokenness and confusion. Throughout the New Testament, this word, *akatharsis,* is juxtaposed with *hypocrisy* (Matthew 23:27), *lawlessness* (Matthew 23:28), *greediness* and *sensuality* (Ephesians 4:19 and Colossians 3:5), and *sexual sin* (Galatians 5:29, Ephesians 5:3, and 1 Thessalonians 4:7). Clearly, being in a state of *akatharsis* is a broken condition where one eventually becomes arrogant, callous, and sexually immoral.

In Romans 1:27 we see that this broken condition now causes these people to *"receive in their own persons the due penalty of their error."*

What is the *error* that was made? No dialogue! They rejected the revelation of God and refused to look up in conversation with Him. What is the *penalty* for that error? No cleansing! The penalty is that we get stuck in *akatharsis,* stuck in being unable to cleanse the heart. The penalty is that you get trapped in a heart of toxic attitudes, and you cannot get spiritually, emotionally, or mentally healthy.

The error: no dialogue.

The penalty: no cleansing.

The result: spiritual sickness, mental confusion, and emotional immaturity leading people to live out Paul's most hideous list of the sins of humanity (Romans 1:29-32).

In monologue we are not self-aware. We continue to speak our own self-deceptions. We cannot cleanse our hearts to get well. We remain stuck in our spiritual progress.

What does monologue sound like? Here's one example: When a woman walks into church and starts talking to herself, saying, *Did I overdress? I should I have worn those other shoes! Oh, look, there's that woman who thinks she's so gorgeous. Where can I sit so I don't have to see her? We should never have moved here. I wish we were back at our old church. These people are not friendly. Oh, great, there's that usher who's always smiling so big and fake. I'll never make any friends here. They won't ever like me. I don't know enough Bible. Yeah, I definitely should have worn those other shoes.*

Evaluate this woman's monologue. She has a boatload of "unfinished business." She has never "finished" the conversations with God about her husband's job and their move to a new city. She has no faith to accept life as it is showing up. In her case, she is in a new church but she has no confidence to make new friends; she is not trusting of others; she is full of doubt, insecurity, self-rejection, rejection of others, victimhood, judgments, a critical spirit, and fear. She is in monologue. She is living in *akatharsis*. She is unclean in her heart's attitudes and judgments. She cannot get well until she acknowledges all of it.

Our monologue creates our wounded and broken shame-based identity. Our monologue causes that identity to become entrenched in our souls. Our monologue reinforces our victimhood; it supports our arrogance; it excuses our rebellion; and it keeps us satisfied that everyone else is wrong about us. Our monologue "tells" us we are right, and it betrays our true identity in Christ.

Our monologue leads us to lose congruency between our beliefs, our values and our behavior. We know that our selfish, sinful behaviors are not God's biblical values; that our behavior is out of line with His word. We know this. But over time we become desensitized. We can't walk congruently with our beliefs, our values, and our behaviors. We then live inconsistent, broken Christian lives.

The Holy Spirit is always ready to start a dialogue with us about our interior condition, to lead us into self-awareness and acknowledgement. For you cannot change or heal what you do not acknowledge.

By the way, this is where addicts learn something about grace that most others do not. The only way to break the power of strongholds and addictive sin is to engage God in a dialogue about all of the "unfinished business" that we carry in our hearts. This unfinished business is what drives our addictions and compulsions. We need dialogue with the Father about our hurts, wounds, rejections, and faulty ways of thinking. We need dialogue about our unforgiveness, bitterness, hatred, and despair. We need to talk with Him and listen to Him.

When we enter into dialogue, He can guide us to acknowledge this brokenness we carry in our hearts. Then in dialogue we start to finish that business. In dialogical prayer, meeting Him in our painful memories, we get comfort for our hurts and wounds; we get words of acceptance from Him for our rejections; and we forgive others and give up roots of bitterness and hatred. The Father talks us into faith, and our despair disappears. We talk through it with Him (and any others that He sends to us) and He cleanses us from all unrighteousness.

Everyone has unfinished business, and sometimes everyone else in the room can see it. Religious people have it, too. But when we dialogue with God, we get healed. When we fight the dialogical fight of grace and faith for our freedom, we find victory. Then we learn something about grace that most others in the church never learn, but need to. In a chapter to come, I will show you how to have this dialogue with God. But let's first set the table more fully. Some of you don't believe the title of my book. You've been trained to believe that God is angry with you for all of these hideous sins that arise out of monologue. But He's not. Let me show you.

CHAPTER 6

God's Not Mad at You!

"God told them, 'I've never quit loving you and never will. Expect love, love, and more love!'"

—Jeremiah 31:3 MSG

We read in the Old Testament that the ground opened up and swallowed people, a fire burned rebellious men to ashes, and the Amalekites were wiped out with no mercy at all, while worriers and whiners were wiped-out in the Wilderness Wandering. Moses didn't get to enter the Promised Land because he hit a rock too many times! Are you kidding? With stories like these, it's not hard to believe that the sins of rebellion and insurrection make God mad.

When the Law of Moses was read to the people in Deuteronomy, God promised curses would come upon the nation if they were disobedient. Sin brought curses. Sin was punished. God even visited the sins of a father on his children and his children's children.

This is the implication, easy to draw, from just a casual reading of the historical books of the nation of Israel: if you sin, God doesn't care what your story is. He's mad!

The theology of the Law of Moses still permeates our New Testament churches and child-rearing today. In our legalistic denominations of Christianity, parents still scold their disobedient child with words like, "Shame on you . . . God's going to punish you for that!" This is a false theology of the Old Covenant, and sadly it is still believed today in many churches.

From the beginning, when Adam and Eve sinned, there is no mention of God being angry. The message in Genesis 3 was not "if you sin, God gets angry." Rather, the message was "sin brings death."

Sin brings death. But God did not open up the ground and swallow Adam and Eve. A fire did not consume them. Instead, God offered the death of animals as a covering for sin, both literally and symbolically, which freed Him to deal graciously with the man and wife. The blood of the animals covered our parents' sin. Then the skin of the animals covered their nakedness. Both were the provisions of grace. Sin brings death, but Grace provides atonement.

From the beginning the truth has been, well, how did the Apostle Paul put it? "Where sin increased, grace abounded all the more" (Romans 5:20). This grace of God was manifest in different ways throughout the Old Testament, but was put on center stage in Yahweh's crowning covenant, the New Covenant. Spelled out in Jeremiah

31:29-34, God assures us that He will forgive us of all our iniquities, and remember our sins no more. This covenant even cancels the former fear that the sins of the father will be visited on the children. Under the New Covenant all sins will be carried away and remembered no more, and those sins will have no visitation rights.

When Jesus showed up to inaugurate the New Covenant, His ministry and teaching were to the effect that the fullness of Grace had come. To the paralytic (Mark 2) He said, "Your sins *are* forgiven." To the woman caught in adultery He said, "I do not condemn you" (John 8). Jesus hung out with sinners, and apparently was not mad at them! In fact, He told them a story to reveal the God of the New Covenant. He told the story of a father who had been told by his own son, "I wish you were dead; now give me my inheritance early, because I'm going to leave the country to go find myself!" (Luke 15, *with a little liberty*!) When the prodigal son had spent it all, he rehearsed a speech all the way home, a speech that his waiting father interrupted. He interrupted his own son trying to repent! That wouldn't sit well in some churches today. For heaven's sake, he interrupted the "repent attempt" with a shout of, "Let's party!" For the father was not angry with either of his sons, though both of them had wasted His kindness and wasted a season of their lives.

God is not mad. How do we know this? He told us He would be this way. He told us in the Old Testament.

Some 700 years before Jesus was born in a manager, Isaiah 53 recorded an amazing prophecy describing Christ's death for our sins—amazing for its descriptive detail of how Jesus would be killed, and what it would mean.

He was struck, beaten, crushed.
He was pierced through for our transgressions,
He was crushed for our iniquities.

Like a lamb that is led to slaughter . . .
He made many to be accounted righteous,
He bore the sin of many . . . "

(Isaiah 53:4,5,7,11,12)

In this astonishing passage, we have the clear prophetic word, hundreds of years in advance, that the Suffering Servant would take our sins away, and we would be made right with God.

Now, let me ask a profound question: *What follows this good news? What follows Isaiah 53?* That's right, Isaiah 54.

What's in the next chapter? The first words are, "Shout for joy!" (NASB), "Break into singing and cry aloud!" (ESV), and "Burst into song, shout for joy" (NIV).

Why? What's up? Why shout for joy? Why start singing?

Well, because of Isaiah 53. Because our sins have been taken away. The Messiah has made a way for us to be counted as righteous. We are forgiven. It's finished! *Twist and shout!*

Further down the passage, the chapter gets even more exciting. Look at verse 9:

*"This is like the days of Noah to Me; as I swore that the waters of Noah should no more go over the earth, **so I have sworn that I will not be angry with you, and I will not rebuke you.**"*

What is like the days of Noah to God? Answer: the days of the substitutionary, atoning death of Christ, the days of Isaiah 53. After God has our sins removed and taken away by Christ, He follows with this amazing revelation: *He will not be angry with us anymore!*

When will He not be angry anymore?

After Isaiah 53. After Christ takes our sins away on the cross, and shares His righteous life with us through the resurrection. After the final Day of Atonement.

This is the import of the New Covenant: **God is no longer mad at us!**

I know you've probably never heard church folks tell you this. We've picked up from others in the pews that God is always disappointed with us. He's frustrated with us for our disobedience, our lack of faith, for not reading our Bibles enough, or for never praying. If He's mad about that stuff, imagine how he feels about our life story of strongholds and sins!

So many of us have been taught to believe that if we sin, then we should not be expecting a blessing from God. Don't be asking for goodies from God if you know He's mad at you!

One man told me, "I used to get so defeated when my pastor would say things like, 'God won't bless you because of that sin; He will put you on the shelf.' I can still hear it in my head today."

We have been taught (wrongly, I assert) to believe that God is ready to get back at us for sinning; thus, this is why bad stuff happens in our lives. Because we have not been as obedient as we should, we interpret the misfortunes in our life as God being disappointed in us. Our cars break down, our washing machines break, we lose a client, or we get a flat tire in the rain—anything like this, we interpret as God trying to teach us a lesson, for He is mad at us.

Our story shames us into believing that we are unworthy, despicable disappointments to God, and so we don't need to be praying and asking Him for anything. Not today. Not until we can lay down a decent track record of obedience, for at least a few days in a row! Our subtle theology that we say to ourselves silently is this: *I sin so bad, so I know He's mad.*

No! His anger was exhausted at the cross. Both the penalty phase and the punishment phase for our sins are over and finished. Christ paid both. If you are a believer in Jesus Christ, then you have received His death for your death, and God is finished punishing anyone for your sins. He chose the cross of Christ to be the focal point of His wrath, and there, at the cross, He finished being *mad* about sins. (I know the Great Tribulation is coming, but I don't plan on being here for it! That judgement is not for His children.) He says He's done. How could we be punished for our sins if He remembers them no more? This issue of our sins is *over and finished.*

However, He is not finished with the transformation of our souls and delivering us from our stories. But He is finished with any *punishment.* He doesn't *approve* of your sins, so He disciplines those He loves (Hebrews 12:5-8). He prunes the branches of the vine (John 15:2), but He does not punish you. Because of Isaiah 53, He's free to deal graciously with you, and He's no longer mad about your sins.

Now, while God is not mad, I'm sorry to say that your sister-in-law *is* mad at your sins. Oh, yeah! Your wife is mad, too, and when she complains to her sister about your sin problem, then you can bet, they are both mad at you. Your brother-in-law, your wife's Bible study teacher, and your wife's other friend, you know, what's-her-name on the worship team—yeah, all of them are mad at you for your sins. Confess your sins at church and half of the congregation will be mad at you! But God never will be.

In fact, look further into this chapter, Isaiah 54:15: *"If anyone stirs up strife against you, **it is not from Me!**"* Other people will be offended by your secret sins when they find out about them. They will be offended, and so they will stir up strife, *but it will not be coming from the Lord.*

Others will terrorize you! They will condemn you! But God doesn't do it. If they fashion weapons against you (verbal assault? slander? accusation? judgment? condemnation? even publish your sin in the church bulletin?!), that weapon will not prevail. Their slander cannot prevail against those who are in Christ Jesus. He is our Righteousness.

God is not mad. Other people might be!

God is finished judging and condemning your sin. Other people might only be getting started! God wants to grow you in righteousness (54:14), but other people just want to bury you in condemnation!

I know this might sound like I am speaking a foreign language. But you can read all of the New Testament epistles, and you will not read about God being mad at you for your sins. The unbeliever is still under the wrath of God (John 3:36; Ephesians 5:6), but not the believer in Christ who has become a child of God.

Romans 5:1 can add to our discussion. It says that we have *peace* with God through the Lord Jesus Christ. ***Peace! Reconciliation. He's not mad.***

Romans 8:1 is dead on. *"There is now no condemnation for those who are in Christ Jesus."* **No condemnation!** That, too, sounds like He's not mad.

Now, for sure, God does have a negative feeling about our sins. The New Testament does give us a glimpse into how God feels about our sins today, on this side of the cross. Paul tells us in Ephesians 4:30, "don't grieve the Holy Spirit." Grief. That's what He feels. Our sin grieves God. Not because it hurts Him, but because He knows how much it is hurting us. He is grieved that in childhood we were bullied, abused, or betrayed, and that we turned from

Him and gave into lusting and craving, eating and drinking, protecting and providing for ourselves. He is grieved that we have stayed in it so long. He is grieved that it has cost us so much. He is grieved that we hurt others with our sins. He grieves, but He is not mad.

But, you might say, *"I keep doing it. I can't quit. Come on, man, I fail over and over, again! How can He not be mad at me for my continual failure?"*

He loves you, anyway, though He is grieved. He is not interested in punishing you, for your sin is doing a mighty fine job of that, already.

Punishment is not on His mind. Transforming you with His Love and Kindness is on His mind. For Paul writes that it is the kindness of God that leads us to repentance, not our fear of His anger (Romans 2:4). More from Isaiah:

> *"The Lord longs to be gracious to you, and therefore, He waits on high to have mercy on you; for the Lord is a God of justice; how blessed are all who long for Him."*
>
> —Isaiah 30:18

God knows your story. Come talk to a God who's not mad at you. Come home to a Father's love. It's time for you, now, to know your story, too. For the truth will set you free, especially the truth about yourself.

THE INNER JOURNEY:

The Discovery
of Shame

CHAPTER 7

Shame: The Blind Spot of Our Interior Condition

"And the Man and the Woman were both . . . not ashamed."

—Genesis 2:24

For many Christians, our stories can have more control over our lives than God does. It's only because we give our stories that kind of significance. We give them that power. Our stories can trap us in shame at an early age in life. At other times, the traps in our story can seem so insignificant that, as we get older, we no longer regard that trap as all that painful. But it could be the birth of our shame. This is why we need a dialogue with God. He knows our story, and He knows where we accepted a shame that has grown into a controlling influence over us.

As I mentioned in the first chapter, I grew up skinny and slow and I was not going to be mistaken for a gifted athlete as a kid. But up until the fifth grade that didn't matter much. All was well in my life, until one day.

One day in the fifth grade something happened in the school cafeteria that changed my life forever, and I knew it would never be the same again. I was sitting at a table for six, which on this day included James, Terry, and Cal. Now, James was the biggest kid in our class. He outweighed all of us. This fact automatically made him the toughest kid in the class, and everyone acknowledged his heavyweight title ranking. I had come to figure that Terry was ranked #2. (I think it was because of the street he lived on.) But Cal? Why shoot, ol' Cal had been my friend since we were five years old. He wasn't tough. He wasn't weak. He was just . . . Cal. So, James was #1. Terry was more than likely #2, and all the rest of us were just there, somewhere beneath them.

James was too big to play on our little league football team, a team where Terry and Cal were starters, and I played left-out. That means, as the skinny kid I would not play, but I would cheer on the others from the bench, left out, while trying to look as tough as possible, you know, just in case anybody on the other team asked about me. I wore number 33, which on reflection today, I marvel that they gave me such a cool number. It was much too slick of a number to be wasted on the skinny kid on the bench. But I wore it proudly, and tried hard to look like a worthy #33.

Now, while sitting at the lunchroom table this day, someone noticed the new kid. He was in the other fifth-grade class. He wore a black, shiny jacket with the emblem of Japan on the back, an emblem stitched in intense, shiny colors of yellow, pink, and green, as I recall. We had an Air

Force base on the edge of town, so perhaps this new kid was the son of an airman.

James spotted him first, "There's that new kid." Terry turned around to look and said, "Yeah, he thinks he's tough with that black jacket." James added, "Yeah, someone ought to beat him up." (And no, that was not the original language he used!) Terry piled on, "Yeah, I would like to beat him up," but then humbly admitted, "but . . . he looks too big. I probably couldn't."

Now wait. Mind you, I've got my head down as this conversation started. I look up to see the boy, but got back quickly to my first addiction: dessert. I was busy, circling the edge of my spoon around the inside of my round dish of vanilla pudding. I loved that stuff. It always came with half-a-cherry on top, which I maneuvered around the dish to allow its survival until the final bite. I enjoyed lunch, and definitely would have preferred the safe, emotional comfort of a lunch table dialogue with buddies who might be discussing what we would do after school at the irrigation ditch. Not on this day. I found myself unexpectedly caught-up in the eternal question that is a rite of passage for adolescent boys: the question of "who-can-beat-up-who?" But there was no discussion as to why it was that a kid with an impressive, shiny, black jacket needed to be beat up at all.

As soon as Terry experienced his moment of humility and confessed that the new kid was too big, and that he probably could *not* beat him up, Cal spoke up. He calmly asserted, "I could beat him up." I figured that he had lost his mind, so I immediately let out a minor guffaw. I laughed, for I thought that if #2 cannot beat up the kid, then none of the rest of us could. I had never thought of Cal's rank among the heavyweight contenders of the world. (The world, at that time, consisted of all the other grade school boys from around town that we encountered around the common grounds of the high school football stadium on Friday nights.) Yet, as I laughed, Terry conceded, "Yeah, Cal, he's too big for me, but you probably could beat him up."

Ohmigosh, what?! Tectonic plates shifted underneath me. Did #2 just yield his throne to Cal? If Cal was now tougher than Terry . . . I realized that . . . that . . . uh, oh . . . I think I just saw a pecking order emerge beyond the count of 2. Could it be that Cal was #2? Terry would be #3. Who then would be #4? And I? Where would I rank in this brave, new world? In a silent panic, I quickly began to scan the other lunch tables, sizing up all the other boys in my fifth-grade class. I saw two other boys that I figured I could beat up. *Whew*, I thought. I don't think I'm at the bottom, but I hoped that I wouldn't have to prove that someday.

Right there in the grade school cafeteria life changed dramatically for me. No one else noticed. The sun went behind a cloud, and I knew life would never be the same again. It wasn't fair. Life had been just fine. I had my vanilla pudding and my piece of cherry. Life had been just fine, up until dessert that day.

I didn't know *his* name, yet, but Masculinity announced his arrival in our lives at lunch that day. In the school cafeteria, Masculinity made a fist and pounded the table. He glared at the new kid in the shiny jacket. He flexed his muscles and winked at the cheerleaders, and I trembled in his presence. For I knew that I didn't measure up to him. I didn't measure up to the brute reality of what it now meant to be worthy and approved. In the presence of Masculinity, I was still a boy, with skinny wrists and little fists. I didn't have adequate artillery. I was weak. Inferior. I didn't measure up, couldn't measure up, and I didn't have a choice about it. Life changed for me, and it would never be the same again. It would mean a problem for me in sports and in other power-rankings with peers, as well as with the girls, as I would later discover. In time, I would make up in my mind that this inferiority meant I would never be acceptable. I would always be ashamed of who I was.

It wasn't fair. I repeat, *It wasn't fair!* I hated it. I hated it, but even worse, I slowly began to hate who I was. I was unworthy of jersey #33. Who was I fooling?

Everyone, I hoped. But I wasn't fooling myself. I knew good and well that I was skinny, weak, and scared. And if proving that you're a man meant fighting and beating up somebody, then I knew that my fists were too small, my wrists too skinny, and my stomach too weak for it. Right then and there, around noon on a winter's day, in the cafeteria of Jefferson Elementary School, shame, like a demon, flew into my heart. Within a few minutes our class got up to take our trays and file out of the cafeteria. Emotionally, I never left that table. Emotionally and psychologically, I sat there at that table for the next thirty years. I had a new identity, based on the shame in my heart, and it had me bound to my lunchroom chair.

My story started an internal dialogue that would soon control my life.

I was just ten years old when this happened. Thirty-two years later I was sitting in a counselor's office trying to figure out how an addiction destroyed my pastoral ministry, and nearly destroyed my family. What had ruined my life?

In that counseling office, I was tasked with the assignment to look back over my life and draw a picture of where this destructive behavior had come from. Where did I begin to hate who I was, and how did I learn to cope with it and comfort myself with a destructive addiction? It was there that this old memory of the lunchroom table came up in my heart. I realized it was the birthplace of shame, and I could now recognize it for its destructiveness. I told my story, and my story told my shame.

Trying to pastor a church without dealing with this shame had brought me to the end of myself. I had been playing a role as "preacher-man," but now my shame and self-protection had caused me to hurt many people. I now saw how it had started. On that day in the counselor's office, I began to change. I began to own my story and heal at the level of identity.

We all have an element of shame in our identity. We got it from our parents, Adam and Eve. If we never acknowledge it, we will never deal with it. For, again, you cannot change or heal what you do not acknowledge, and most Christians don't really know what their shame is, or where it comes from.

I didn't know where mine came from, and it destroyed my ministry. Our pews, our pulpits, and our leadership teams are filled with those of us who do not know how shame is manifesting in hurtful and painful relationships. Therefore, we never find healing grace, and our transformation stops way short of maturity. This is the crisis in our churches today.

CHAPTER 8

Shame is an Identity

"Shame is a soul-eater."

—C.G. Jung

My friend, Dave, was a headmaster at a Christian school. One day there was a small scandal when some of the seventh grade boys were caught cheating on an exam. Oh, my! Cheating at the Christian school. In a short time all of the boys but one confessed. One student tried to weasel his way out of being disciplined, as he tried to deny that he had cheated. The principal for the Junior High students eventually took this young boy into her private office to confront him. Dave stood outside her closed door to eavesdrop and listen in on her interrogation. Inside her office the principal challenged the young man over and over until finally he broke down and confessed that, yes, he had cheated. "Aha!" she said, "So, you're a liar." She wore him down and the truth came out.

Later, Dave had a private conversation with this principal. He challenged the conclusion of her efforts with the young man. Dave said, "Instead of concluding that he lied, you called him a liar. You went beyond gaining his confession. You declared his identity."

She shamed him. She labeled him a liar. It would have been better for her to say, "You are a beloved child of God and all of your teachers love you, but today you betrayed your true life in Christ by cheating and then lying about it." But instead of merely calling out his sins, she declared his identity: Liar.

I wonder if at that moment, shame, like a demon, flew into his heart.

A childhood name or accusation can stick for a long time. James says that the tongue is like a fire! It can set the course for your life, or someone else's life, for the tongue is set on fire by Hell (James 3:6). Did your parents, a teacher, best friends, or a bully destroy your heart with a word? Does your story contain someone's words of disapproval, disdain, or destruction, proclaiming an identity over you?

The shame of your story has its origin in another true story, the first story. As we pointed out in Chapter 1, Shame was birthed under a tree in the Garden of Eden. Adam and Eve had been naked in front of each other, and completely comfortable and fully accepting of one another. Genesis 2:24 reads, "And the man and the woman were both naked and not ashamed." Naked with no shame. But after they ate from the Tree, shame came. They lost that self-acceptance and casual comfortableness, and were no longer comfortable in their own skin. They covered up their bodies, specifically where they were different from one another. They hid their nakedness, and then they hid from God.

This is *Shame*: the inability to accept yourself and be comfortable in your own skin; the fear that you will somehow be "revealed and seen" for who you are, and then no longer be accepted and loved. Shame is shot through with fear, too. For Adam, it included the fear of "the Woman" as well as the fear of God. Shame is no mere feeling or passing emotion. Shame is an identity. You build it around your failures, scandals, and sins, as well as the judgments you make against yourself. Shame also comes from the wounds, rejections, and sins of others. Indeed, it can even come from the internal discomfort in your heart from breaking your agreements and promises.

Shame is why we have this instinctive *need for acceptance* in the deepest part of our being. We want to be wanted. We want to be loved. We want to be acceptable. We hate to fail and disappoint others. We hate how we think and feel about ourselves when we are empty, wounded, and rejected by others. We hate to be exposed. This is Shame, and the loneliness and emptiness of it is what drives our stories.

There is a difference between Shame and Guilt. Guilt is when I do something wrong, and I acknowledge that I made a mistake and now need to apologize to the offended party. Guilt sounds like this: "Oh, no, look what I've done! I've really made a mistake! I will need to apologize and make amends. I hope they will not be too upset. I will go back and make this right." In Guilt, I can stand apart from my mistake. My mistake and I have separate identities. I am not the mistake, I merely made one.

Shame sounds more like this: "Aw, crud! I'm so stupid! Look what I've done, this time. I've really blown it; look at this mess. They're going to hate me. Now I've got to go and apologize. I'm such an idiot; I hate myself." In Shame I cannot stand apart from my mistake. My mistake and I do not have separate identities. For I didn't just make a mistake, I *am* a mistake-maker!

This is Shame, and it is not merely a feeling. Guilt is a feeling, but **Shame is an identity.** It is a mental picture in my heart of my value, goodness, and power in this world, and it runs from my head to my toes. It forms my soul in the image of self-hatred.

S-H-A-M-E: Self Hatred Against ME. At the core of Shame is the loss of self-acceptance and self-respect. Shame is a like a swimming pool with a shallow end, a middle, and a deep end.

Shallow Shame

On the shallow end of the pool, Shame is merely *"the inability to accept some things about myself."* Shallow Shame is the kind of shame where a well-dressed man, successful in his career, respected by friends and co-workers, still has a haunting, nagging dislike of himself. Many successful people don't like the fact that they are too demanding of themselves, too emotional, too angry, too controlling of others, or sometimes just too selfish. Despite their outward success, these people might secretly believe they are unworthy of their success.

In this shallow level of shame you are wrestling with some rejection about your physical appearance. You dislike the fact that you're too tall, or you're too short; your ears are too long, or your nose is too long; your neck is too long, or your toes are too long. You're too fat; you're too skinny. You're too fair-skinned or freckled; and your hair is too thin or too curly. You can't measure up to the marvelously endowed and pigmented Kardashians, so you don't like the way that you look. Doesn't everyone have some element of Shame at this shallow level?

Middle Shame

In the middle of the pool, a little deeper, is a second level of shame. This level of Shame is *"a lack of self-respect and self-care."* This is where you have a deeper dislike of yourself, and you demonstrate that you do not respect yourself. At this level of Shame, you struggle more internally with emotional and mental conflicts because you judge yourself as unworthy and unacceptable.

You're not smart enough, not cool enough, not clever enough, or not promotable enough. You never feel the approval of your approved peers, so you disrespect yourself. You sleep too much, don't read enough, or don't finish many things you start, so you call yourself lazy.

Your reports are not thorough enough, your sales numbers are not high enough, or your suggestion at staff meeting wasn't thought through enough, so you tell yourself you are never good enough.

To cope, you pick up new comforting behaviors (eating too much; drinking too much, or some sort of sexual behavior . . . too much!). Of course, these behaviors now tell you that you are a disappointment to God and others.

At this level of Shame you want to lose weight, but you never do. You hold back from participating in some activity where you know you will not be successful, fearing ridicule or even failure. You belittle yourself when you make a mistake. You call yourself a mild invective, like "dummy." You laugh at yourself in front of others, but the laugh is a way of deflecting your deeper embarrassment and disapproval of yourself.

Deep Shame

At the deep end of the pool of Shame is a third level, "Self-Hatred." Those of us down at this end of the pool have shame that is over our heads. We are drowning in it. We reject ourselves, and our behavior is definitely destructive. When we make a mistake we unmercifully berate ourselves, castigate ourselves, and call ourselves, "stupid idiot, dumb*ss," or far worse. We are full of mental and emotional pain, and our goal in life is to distract ourselves from ever feeling it. We can't fix our own pain, so we cause others to join us in our pain. At this level of shame we are flagrantly judgmental, critical, and offensive, and often with no filter on our mouth. We reject others before they reject us.

At this end of the pool are many of those who have been abused by others. When children are physically, emotionally, or sexually abused, they grow up to hate who they are, and often grow up to abuse others. In their self-hatred they do behaviors that are unloving and cruel to themselves, as well as to others. Their self-destructive ways demonstrate their shame.

Addicts actually hate themselves. Their self-destructive behaviors are abusive, and they know it. I've asked men addicted to pornography if they love themselves. They usually reply that they do. But I know they don't, so I ask them if they love their sons. They reply, "Of course." Then I ask, "Would you ever teach your son how to look at porn as a way of dealing with his own emotional pain?" They look at me like I'm crazy, and say, "Of course not, that's not the loving thing to do!" I let the irony linger in the air and then ask, "So then, you don't really love yourself either, do you?"

Deepest Shame

But there is yet still a deeper level of Shame. As destructive as it is staying afloat in addiction at the deep end of the pool of shame, it is even worse to sink to the bottom of the pool. Down at the drain is Shame at the level of *"Self-rejection."* At this level, people are abusing drugs, abusing alcohol, indulging pornography addictions, and more to the damage of their brain and soul. This level can even include people addicted to piercings and tattoos, or addicted to extreme plastic surgery, modifying and altering their appearance to look like objects other than a human.

At the bottom of the pool of Shame are those who participate in self-injury, the person who pierces, cuts, and self-flagellates. This person's warped shame knows no relief from emotional pain, so they attempt to use the *ebbing relief of the physical pain* as a substitute. It is as if the person is trying to create a physical pain that they can then comfort, as a substitute for comforting the emotional pain that they no longer feel.

When Shame Begins to Heal

Whichever level of Shame you live in, your tendency will be to move toward self-protection and avoidance. When you are unable to accept yourself, then the tendency will be to ignore the conversations going on in your head. Because of fear, you will never "listen" to the truth that is being spoken in your mind.

First, you fear acknowledging to yourself what you suspect to be true. For then you will have to hold yourself accountable for changing this. You will not be able to blame other people, now. These fears are the structure of your Shame. Failing to deal with your shame at this level, of course, can lead you deeper into the Pool.

We must begin to listen to the story that our Shame is telling us. The story of our failures; the story of our scandals and sins; the story of the damage other people have done to us; and the story of our self-judgments.

These stories are trying to tell us we need healing. We must learn our story of Shame, and we must tell it. We need to tell our story to safe people. For in telling our story, we will *begin* a deep inner journey toward four works of grace in our hearts. In telling our story we *begin* the journey to:

- better understand it;
- get healing from it;
- find freedom from it;
- and gain power over it.

Healing, freedom, and power are the spiritual discoveries that come from a deep inner journey, a journey rooted in dialogue. Let's now look more closely at the elements of our story that must be told and understood.

CHAPTER 9

The Process of Shame

"Though this be madness, yet there is method in it."

—Polonius to self, regarding Hamlet

As we grow up, we create a shame-based identity, built around our wounds, our sins, and our secrets. This identity is based on the shame we feel and believe about ourselves. Did you notice the vocabulary words I used in the earlier chapters about my story? Skinny. Weak. Fearful. Inadequate. This was my vocabulary of shame, and it arose out of the hurtful events in my life: when a bully called me names, when a friend exposed my weaknesses, when a teacher humiliated me in front of the class. My shame started with my painful story, but it grew worse with the scripting in my mind.

You see, it's not merely that we have a painful story. The defeat in our story grows worse from the fact that we are *Meaning-Making-Minstrels*. We do even more damage to our hearts by the songs we sing to ourselves, about ourselves.

After we experience painful, hurtful events in life, we then make up in our minds that those events *mean something* far worse and terrible. We give these painful events too much significance and power over us. Over time, we weave the *meanings* into a song for our lives, and we sing it to ourselves. After David killed Goliath and even more Philistine militia, the children of Israel made up a song about their hero and his score, and they sang it in the streets of Israel (1 Samuel 18:6-7). But Saul, feeling humiliated, sang a different song in his heart. His song *meant* that he was a failure. It was the song of a coward. His song to himself led to an identity of shame, and to emotional depression (1 Samuel 18:8-10).

There is a process to our madness, and it goes something like this. Growing up we experience all kinds of hurtful and painful events. Some of these events are milder, but, of course, some events are traumatic and scandalous. These are the kinds of painful events that cause us to lie in bed every night for the next several days, maybe weeks, and think about that event over and over. We relive the trauma of the event in our mind again and again, but as we replay the scene in our mind something terrible happens: a *meaning* emerges. A *deep conviction* settles on us, and we are convinced that the *meaning* we are telling ourselves is beyond dispute. We become convinced that this event means, for example, *I'll never be good enough, or I am stupid; I'm a reject, or I'm no one's priority; I'm unwanted, or I'm alone and no one cares; love will be scarce in my life; I'll never be loved, or I will never be loved the way I want to be loved.* The conclusion we draw from this meaning, this deep conviction is that *I am unable to accept myself.* This is the shallow end of the pool of shame, and our self-talk gives birth to our shame-based Identity.

Since I believe now that I don't measure up, or that I'm not valuable enough, I must begin posing and posturing *as if I do* measure up. I must fool everyone so that they don't also come to see and believe that I am inadequate or in any way unacceptable. From the *meaning* that has emerged in my heart, I now develop *a purpose-driven life.* That's right, long before we ever read the book with that title, we had one already. We always have had a purpose-driven life, for better or for worse. Based on the deep convictions (the *meanings)* we believe about ourselves, we decide on a way to live so as to hide these painful convictions in our hearts.

In Psalm 139:3, David says that God knows *"my path and my lying down, and He is intimately acquainted with all my ways."* The words for *path* and *lying down* are words that speak of a course for living, a life-direction, even a career path. David is saying that God knows his *purpose-driven life.* God knows the posing and posturing *paths* that David has chosen for his life.

It's the same for us today. Once I decide my convictions, my *meanings,* are true (e.g., that I am worthless, or a reject, or that I don't measure up), I now must fool everyone to think the opposite. Thus, I choose a path for acting that out. I choose where I will "lie down." My hobbies, my activities, my friends, my major in college, my taste in boyfriend or girlfriend, my clothing style and the type of car I drive, even my career choices and the reasons for leaving or staying at a job—all are based on this conviction of who I believe I am, and what I need for managing my image. I develop my life according to this one purpose: to not be exposed as the unacceptable person that I am convinced I am.

After that moment in the school cafeteria, I would lie in bed and think about that moment over and over again. Over a few days and weeks I came to the conclusion that if my wrists are too skinny and my fists are too small, then my purpose in life must be to avoid getting in a fight. To avoid getting in a fight, I must then be the kind of guy that no one wants to punch in the face. Whom do you not want to punch in the face but the friendly, nice guy! As well, no one ever wants to punch the funny guy and make him cry. So, my purpose-driven life became this: be the funny, nice guy, and make no enemies.

Out of my fears I developed *a false self,* a new personality to present to the hostile world I lived in. I became the friendly guy who (just naturally!) is funny and nice. I created someone who lived outside of my true self.

Out of this *false self* I then developed a corresponding life *walking according to the flesh.* I began to be a people-pleaser. I let others have their way, and gave up my own desires. I gave up my right to have a voice. I never talked back to anyone; I always complimented with phony sweetness, and I never created an enemy. This meant that often I had to eat dirt and let others have their way, take advantage of me, or even push me around. I had to lower my competitiveness, and sometimes act disinterested. Even with girls, the ones I had a crush on would tell me they loved me like a brother, which was certainly frustrating. Today, I understand, for who would want to be the girlfriend of the classroom coward!

Naturally, deep down inside I grew angry, very angry, as I saw everyone as a bully, and I saw myself as a victim. Of course, I couldn't let the anger out because that might lead to a fight, which I must avoid at all costs! By the time I finished high school, I was the perfect kind of guy to go to Bible college—I was a nice guy, outwardly seeming a perfect fit for the ministry, yet completely unaware of how much anger I carried inside myself.

Later on, during my seminary days I took a personality test. The score for my Anger quotient nearly shot off the top of the chart! My anger graded at the highest level. The counselor pointed that out and he figured it was an anomaly because, well, he knew me as such a nice guy! I agreed, of course. *"An anomaly. Oh, absolutely. For sure. It must be,"* I told him. *"I'm not angry like that!"* The next quotient score, however, was for Gentleness. I scored in Gentleness nearly as high as I scored in Anger. Ah, no wonder my anger didn't reveal itself so terribly. My gentleness covered it up. I didn't understand it at that time, so I shrugged my shoulders.

Fifteen years later in counseling for my own addiction I recalled that test I had taken back in seminary. The anger, it turns out, was not an anomaly. I *was* that angry; however, the anger was being masked by the phony gentleness. God was giving me an insight into my heart back in seminary, but I missed it. I remained content to keep living my *purpose-driven life*, hiding my anger and living the *false self* as a gentle, funny, nice guy, friend of all—the profile of the "perfect" pastor!

A man in my church once said to me, "As the pastor goes, so goes the congregation." (Gulp!) I thought I was covering my shame, but I was actually developing and honing my false self. If I was not going to confront *my* shame-based Identity, then I certainly wasn't going to call attention to *your* shame-based identity. No sir, at my church, we were all just going to have Bible studies and small group fellowship. None of this psycho-babble about the journey of the heart. Let's just all be nice.[3] Like the pastor.

This is repeated in churches all across America. Many lay leaders and their pastors are living and leading from a wounded past. That is, they are still carrying the shame from wounds of the past, and acting out of their shame-based Identity. With their flesh-patterns they then create for their viewing audience a false self to hide behind. They received Grace for their salvation (justification), but have never experienced the greatness of Grace that can heal them and take them to new levels of transformation.

---

[3] Parenthetically, do you know where the word *"nice"* comes from? In ancient Latin it had the connotation of a "know nothing." In old French it meant "simple; silly," and in Medieval English it was "foolish, stupid." Therefore, to be a "nice" person is to be an empty fool.

Deep Ministers to Deep

The way of discovering this deeper work of Grace is to pray and ask God to *"search my heart, see if there be any hurtful way in me . . . "* (Psalm 139:23-24). The *hurtful way* would be this phony, inauthentic Christian life. In dialogue with God I must acknowledge the painful events in my life and the shame-based meaning I gave those events. I must begin to recognize my *Shame-Based Identity*. Then I must acknowledge the fleshly strategy that became my *purpose-driven life*, the strategy to get love and acceptance without being exposed. This strategy became the hurtful way of the *false self*. In my own story, these were my revelations from God:

> My Shame-based identity: *emasculated, inadequate, coward.*
>
> My Purpose-Driven Life: *fleshly strategy of being the funny, nice guy.*
>
> My False Identity: *Friend to All,* that after seminary became, *Preacher Man.*

If we ever get well, we will have to start a dialogue with God with the Psalm 139:24 prayer. Do you know your story? Can you recall the wounds in your heart, and who hurt you? Do you know the identity you have built around your shame? Are you aware of the way of your posing and posturing? Next, can you be honest about and own your fleshly strategies by which you have sought to get your needs met for love and acceptance? Finally, will you identify and renounce the godless, false self you walk in that only has a form of godliness, but is full of self-serving and self-promotion?

When addicts get well, they do so because they finally do this work. They get help and guidance with their shame from someone at the treatment center who has done their shame work. They find a greater grace (James 4:8) on the way to healing and deliverance from their strongholds. Most Christians do not get that desperate enough with their sins. But they should. Let's look at how it's hurting us in the church.

CHAPTER 10

Crisis in the Church: Our Shame, Flesh, and the False Self

"There's a crisis in our churches —-our people are not being dynamically transformed."

—Anonymous Pastor

S hame is Satan's greatest tool of destruction in the church. In Genesis it says that God *"blessed the man and the woman . . . and they were naked and not ashamed"* (Genesis 1:28; 2:25). Apparently, Satan's agenda has been to *curse* the man and the woman, so that they are *clothed* and full of shame. Here's another way it happened to me.

When I finished seminary this funny, nice-guy, friend-of-all became the assistant pastor of a wonderful church. I loved this church. I loved the people, and I loved the senior pastor with whom I worked. The years started off with joy and enthusiasm, as I was well complimented and praised for my service to the Body.

Three years into my service there, I met my wife, Cindy. (Well, you know, she wasn't my wife when I met her.) Life changed quickly. We had a daughter. Then we had a son. Then came the new puppy. Then stains on the carpet. Then chewed-up furniture. Then my orderly life was ruined. Then I got depressed.

Yep, pretty much in that order.

My orderly life changed so dramatically that it gave way to a "walking" depression; the kind of depression you can manage without others noticing. I was motivated by my work at the church, and so I managed enough energy for the day, but when I got home at night, I was withdrawn and silent, with nothing to give to my family. In fact, I remember during that season of life I came home one evening around 7:30 from an elder board meeting. My wife looked at me sheepishly, and said, "I hate to show you this, but . . ." and she pointed to a corner on the kitchen wall where our new puppy had torn the wall-paper. I just looked at it, and didn't say a word. With more "ruin" in my life, I turned and walked to our bedroom, set down my briefcase, fell across the bed fully clothed, and fell into an emotionally exhausted, sound sleep. I did not wake up until the next morning, nearly twelve hours later.

I was depressed. I was unhappy. I thought marriage and family would be different, you know, like—happier. I was miserable. *How did my life go so wrong?* I silently wondered. Gee-whiz, I went to a prestigious Christian college and I was popular. I was a leader in my campus organization. Then I went to seminary and caught the eyes of the professors with an article I wrote in the seminary newspaper; they marveled at my philosophy degree and background. I was an award-winning graduate for my master's thesis. While in seminary I was invited on to the part-time staff of one of the largest, most prestigious churches in the city. Then, after seminary, I joined the personal team of the most popular campus speaker in the world at the time. Now as an assistant pastor, I was starting up ministries the church had never seen before. I was growing adult ministry to the high praise of the Elder Board and the congregation.

I was heading places.

I was good.

I was a superstar, a legend in my own mi—

Oooops. That's right. In my own mind I was overly inflated, thinking more highly of myself than I should. Violating Romans 12:3, I was running on the energy of my good, well-educated, and winsome, people-pleasing flesh. Wait a minute you might say, *"I thought you were developing a shame-based identity. How could you now be so arrogant and self-promoting?"* Oh, I was operating at church in my False Self. All of that arrogance and self-promotion was the posing and posturing of the False Self, the "Award-Winning Preacher Man." Remember, the false self is the fool we send out in public to put on a show, so that no one finds out how ashamed we feel on the inside.

But now, only a few years into my work as an assistant pastor and so early into marriage, I was depressed. The shift in my life from carefree, single man to responsible assistant pastor, husband, and father was more difficult than I thought it would be. I thought that my unhappiness was my family's fault. Years later, I would discover that I was depressed at this time in my life because I was a self-centered, selfish addict, full of shame, who wouldn't acknowledge it.

But the real reason for my depression was never dealt with at that time, because I couldn't be honest. For if I had acknowledged my addiction, then I would have lost the privilege of being right, and award-winning seminary graduates have a deep need to be right! I needed to be right about my complaint that other people were the reason for my depression.

Shame will always claim, "someone else is ruining my life."

And that may be the biggest complaint down at church, the complaint of Shame: *others are ruining my life!* This shame-based complaint has caused people to leave churches, split churches, hijack board meetings in churches, steal control in churches, steal money from churches, and even steal the spouse of other church members.

Shame is the gasoline that drives *the flesh.* If you have a compulsive behavior, a regular, automatic behavior that is self-centered and self-serving—that you cannot stop, don't want to stop, or always whip out and use on others—*that* is your flesh. Beneath your behavior you will discover that somewhere in childhood your shame was birthed in some painful memory, some event in life which gave you a message of disapproval about yourself. Pain came to fill your heart as a child. Like a demon, shame flew into your heart. The next thing you began to do was develop some kind of self-centered behavior in an attempt to comfort yourself and control others, to protect yourself from any more pain filling your heart. This behavior became your own unique version of the flesh.

Just like people with an addiction, most Christians, too, have some compulsive, unbroken manner of behavior or attitude that they will not stop. They are deeply committed to it. They do this behavior repeatedly. Automatically! They do this behavior to provide comfort and control for themselves, *just like an addict.* In fact, these people don't realize they are more committed to this particular pattern of behavior than they are committed to walk in righteousness. *Just like an addict.* And when the pastor does preach on point to their sin, these people kick into a mode of denial or rationalization. *Just like an addict.* Then they minimize the negative impact of their behavior. *Just like an addict.*

Of course, the compulsive behavior of a drug or alcohol addiction can get dangerous and destructive. But the other compulsive people in the church? Well, their shame-based behavior is not so dangerous, so they don't do anything about theirs! Here again, those of us who have struggled with addiction have learned something about grace that those without self-awareness might never learn.

It has been my observation that every one of us in church is committed to some disposition, attitude, or behavior, by which we protect ourselves, provide for ourselves, promote ourselves, or control others. We are as diligently devoted to these patterns as any good alcoholic or drug addict, and we are doing it for the same reason they are: to hide our shame. Each of us has our own unique version of Shame, and we desperately cling to our own unique flesh-patterns to try to cover it up.

We cover our shame, but we don't confront it!

My observation is substantiated by the high number of church dropouts. So many Christians, have you noticed, quit growing spiritually after the first few years. They don't realize what is killing their spirituality, so they never get the help they need. They never realize that deep-seated shame and the flesh patterns of their false self are choking out their spiritual growth. Then these people drop out of church.

One problem is that our discipleship programs leave this much deeper spiritual work *unfinished*, at best, or completely *untouched*, at worst.

Discipleship books usually focus on right doctrine and theology, or apologetics and witnessing. We focus on the disciple's Sunday-School-head, but not on his vulnerable, pain-filled heart. Our discipleship models almost never deal with the root issues of the "interior condition" of the disciple.

Some men's material will adequately talk about a father-wound, for instance, but most men need a guide to do their own work around a father-wound. You probably are not going to get healed of a father-wound by hearing one lecture in a football stadium, or by participating only one time in a small group discussion of the topic.

This work—*on the interior condition*—does not get addressed, I think, because so many leaders have never done their own work. They have not had anyone lead them to see their own shame-based identity. So here is what the Christian life is like for so many: they make feeble attempts to change what they can change, in their own strength, as their duty to God, and they never go beyond that.

To confront this interior condition, you will have to confront your stronghold thinking. To confront your stronghold thinking you will have to confront your past and the painful events that caused your shame. But most people avoid the past because there is pain back there, so they avoid the dialogue with God that would lead to a breakthrough.

The next problem is that most strongholds are so deeply embedded in our hearts, that we can't imagine that "the way I live is not the right way." *Are you kidding? You mean, Jesus wouldn't deal with my spouse the way I'm doing it?* At the counseling center where I work, our most difficult clients are the super-religious people who are sent to us by their pastors. When you try to counsel religious people who have been in the church all of their lives, they look at us in disbelief, like, "What? You're telling me that I'm doing something wrong? You're telling me that the problem in my marriage is me?" Religious people hide behind their performance and duty, but are not so willing to acknowledge and deal with their shame-based identities or their false selves.

In the church, for instance, some of us are self-absorbed complainers and we wear our martyrdom ribbons on our chest. We work the crowd to get pity. Every pastor knows that this person will be straight up the aisle after the sermon to drain the rest of his energy. The pastor knows who you are, but he is too kind to confront you. So, you are never forced to acknowledge your unique version of martyr-flesh.

Others of us in the church are victims. We work to get people on our side, and against our alleged enemies. We've done it all of our lives. We are committed to that behavior, *just like an addiction.*

Others of us in the church conceal our weakness in passivity and aloofness to never risk failure, again. Others of us brag to appear more important in the hopes of getting an assignment from the pastor—just as we've done all our lives with teachers, coaches, and bosses.

We are bossy and aggressive to control the committee decisions; or we privately manipulate others to influence our pet decision from the board meeting we just left. We are loquacious to cover up ignorance, and pass judgments to sound superior. We are vindictive to get you before you get us, or act all kind and apologize to play the phony nice guy. We act disinterested so as not to participate with the group in something that might expose our weakness; or we act contrary just to be a problem, because we don't want others to get their way so easily.

Some of us lead a movement to change the leader's plans so as to get our way; or we start a subcommittee to get the leader fired. Husbands never deal with the root issues of their anger and thus keep on wounding their wives. Wives never deal with the root issues beneath their disrespectful undermining of their husband's leadership. *Whoops, now don't put the book down, just because I'm preachin' good!*

You do all of this behavior faithfully. Daily. Weekly. Just like an addict uses his tricks, you are using yours. You addictively do some behavior that you use to control, because you believe that's what God would have you do. You tell everyone down at church, whoever will listen to your story, and whoever will then understand, that you just *had to do what you did, for you had no other choice!*

You are dedicated and devoted to controlling others. So, you are not controlled by the Holy Spirit. But the church will never call you on it, because everyone else is doing his or her own version of the same dance. Church leaders are dancing, too. After one pastor nearly split his second church, one of his friends conceded, "Well, he does have his Achilles heel." Achilles heel, my foot! That pastor has never dealt with his shame-based identity and his false self as "super pastor," complete with flesh patterns for controlling himself, controlling others, and ultimately controlling God!

We tolerate *the flesh* in the church because we aren't bothered enough to confront it. Thus, believers live nearly their entire Christian life, decades in the church, and never change this behavior! They need to, but they won't. Therefore, they never learn what addicts learn about grace and transformation. For addicts, our behavior is so destructive that we might either die or kill somebody if we don't change. But since no behavior mentioned above will cause someone's death, those who walk in these patterns rarely confront their stronghold behavior.

God is not a part of any of this behavior. It is our own creation. We are covering our shame—like in the Garden of Eden—but we never acknowledge that we are hiding!

Finding Grace

I found grace in my darkest hour—a greater grace. It began with a revelation in my heart from Christ one day. Sometime late in the first year of counseling, He opened my eyes to see that I was "chief of all sinners" (1 Timothy 1:15). This was not my true identity, but the Father was showing me that this is who I am apart from Him when I walk in my flesh. God did this because addicts always minimize their sins. But not just addicts. Regular people in the pews do the same. All of us want to minimize how badly we sin, and how badly we need to change.

I was chief of all minimizers. I would not ever admit how bad my problem was, of course, until I got busted. Then I stood there in utter despair, ashamed of myself.

Before I could walk in the newness and the power of my identity in Christ, it was necessary for God to show me that, apart from Him, I was not just a minimal sinner. I was chief of all sinners. After acknowledging that description, I was ready to learn how to live in my true identity.

THE INNER LIFE:

What Most Christians Don't Know About Identity

CHAPTER 11

IDENTITY: The Difference Between Spirit and Soul

Don't spend your whole life trying to become who you already are!

E rin came to see me, and she was emotionally bankrupt. Worn-out. She sat down and began to tell a tale of woe. Her son was struggling with drugs and a personality disorder, but living and working halfway across the country with an inner-city mission. She had come to check on her son's well-being and situation, when the local pastor in whose home she was staying sent her to me thinking that I could be of help to her.

She was also separated from her husband, who on several occasions over the life of their marriage had physically put his hands on her. However, the good news was that late in life, at the present time, he had finally started getting some counseling for his anger. He was doing much better emotionally and spiritually these days, but he definitely had not spent enough time in his own recovery. It was still too soon for him to be doing what he was now doing: pressuring Erin to move back home. This was causing more stress on her.

So, she was living alone at her mother's house. Her husband is prematurely announcing his healing. Her son had been struggling up and down for a couple of years, now. Her daughters were also growing weary of all the drama, and wanting Mom to move back home, too. I wondered where she got such stamina, such fortitude, to stand so courageously in the face of this mess.

As we talked I found out. It only looked like courage. She was closer to the emotional emptiness of a mannequin.

The rest of her story began like this. Erin was the daughter of a state trooper, an officer of the law. Though her parents often bickered, like any other couple, Erin had no idea that her parent's marriage was in any deep trouble. One day, while home from college, Erin was summoned to the kitchen by her alarmed sister. It was the middle of the day, and it was not unusual to see their dad swing by the house in his squad car; however, on this day, dad was moving boxes and clothing out of his bedroom. He was the one who had summoned the sisters to the kitchen. After his car was packed, he came back into the kitchen one last time to announce to his daughters that he was leaving their mother and ending their marriage. Erin was the older sister, and the one emotionally closer to their father. He commissioned her to be the one to announce his departure to their mother when she comes home from work. The Trooper was leaving, and he needed Erin to be his "little trooper" and take charge of the rest of the story at home.

A few hours later when Mom arrived home, Erin and her sister met her in the kitchen. Erin told her that Dad had left. Moved out. Packed up and gone. Her mother was initially in disbelief. "Surely, he's not gone for good," she said. "If his coffee cup is gone, then I'll know he was serious." Mom moved around the kitchen table to the cabinet and opened the door to see his coffee cup. It was gone. Erin stood by helplessly as she watched her mother's shoulders slump and her head drop as her knees buckled. Her mother sunk several inches in stature as reality numbed her heart.

Erin knew what her job was at that moment. She must be that "little trooper" for her mother. Her mother went into a walking depression that lasted for months and months. Erin became the strong one. She was the one to hold things together, as the caretaker, the adult in the house, the leader for this season of great sadness. She did not take a break for her own grief. She became (drum roll, please) . . . "Trooper Girl."

A False Self.

A False self who learned to shut down her own intimacy needs, and be there for everyone else.

Her Shame-based identity now labeled her, *Discounted*. This label told her, "*Your needs are not important as the adults in your life, so take care of us and others; no one will be there for you, though.*"

It was Trooper Girl who showed up at my office that day, now managing the high drama of her own family. She wasn't courageous. She wasn't an amazing woman of faith. She was an emotionless, worn-out child of God. A soldier for her son and his addiction issues, flying across the country to manage his situation; a heart-broken mother who missed seeing her daughters daily since she had not lived at home for nearly a year; and a surrogate mother to her man-child husband as she resisted moving home and insisted on his fuller recovery.

Erin and I had a powerful session together in my office. What we talked about centered on her Identity, her life in her spirit.

Soul vs. Spirit

There is a difference between your spirit and your soul. If you do not understand this, then you will never understand New Testament spirituality. Worse, you will spend your whole life trying to become who you already are. Let me explain.

We are spirit-beings. Our *nature*, our *essence*, our *identity* is spirit. These three words all mean the same thing. To speak of one's nature, is to speak of one's essence, and is to speak of one's identity. Your nature/essence/identity is that which is permanent and unchanging about you. Your identity is what you are and cannot *not* be. That is, if you take the identity of something out of that something, then that something will no longer be that thing!

Our identity is spirit. We are spirit-beings. If you take the spirit out of humans then we would be mere animals. We would have the same soul-ish nature as our pet dogs. What separated us at Creation from the animal kingdom is that God made us in His image. He made us spirit-beings.

Spirit and Soul

I have this on good authority. Genesis 1:26-27 and James 3:9 say that all mankind is made in the image of God. All human beings—believers and unbelievers, Jews and Gentiles—all are made in the image of God.

Then, in John 4, when Jesus was talking to that woman at the well, He told her that God is spirit. Therefore, if we are made in God's image and He is spirit, then we are spirit-beings, too. This is the most fundamental notion of what it means to be made in the image of God. We are spirit-beings. Spirit is our identity. Spirit is our nature. It is what is permanent and unchanging about us. Here is how Peter said it, *"For this is why the gospel was preached even to those who are dead, that though judged in the flesh the way people are, **they might live in the spirit the way God does,**"* (1 Peter 4:6).

As a spirit-being, when I believe and receive the Lord Jesus Christ as my Savior, then I receive His life. I receive God's life into my spirit. Then I *live in the spirit the way God does.*

But my *soul* did not receive the life of God. Not at the moment of saving-faith. God's life came only into my spirit, not my soul, for there is a difference between my spirit and my soul. My spirit was born-again instantly, but my soul is still in need of renewing and transformation on a daily basis. This renewal and renovation of the soul is the major work of a Christian for the rest of life on Earth. This distinction between spirit and soul can ... from the New Testament.

1 Thessalonians 5:23 distinguishes the three dim... of body, soul, and spirit.

> *"Now may the God of peace Himself sanctify you completely, and may your whole **spirit and soul and body** be kept blameless at the coming of our Lord Jesus Christ."*

In our casual thinking as Christians, spirit and soul are never quite separated from one another as we so easily separate soul and body. However, spirit and soul are clearly distinguished from each other, too. Hebrews 4:12 tells us that the Bible can penetrate so deeply into our interior that it can divide between the spirit and the soul:

> *"For the word of God is living and active, sharper than any two-edged sword, piercing to **the division of soul and of spirit,** of joints and of marrow, and discerning the thoughts and intentions of the heart."*

Soul and spirit are different and distinct, in the same way that our physical bones are distinct from the marrow in the bone, and in the same way that our thoughts are distinct from our deeper intentions in the heart.

Further, this passage is teaching that while we are submitting ourselves to reading the Bible, the spiritual power of it can penetrate deeply and reveal to us whether our thinking is of the spirit or of the soul (i.e., *spirit or flesh*).

hessalonians 5:32 indicate
:t from each other. *This is*
not recognize that there is a
and the soul, then I contend
ching on spirituality will never
ance, how would you reconcile
Be transformed by the renewing
of your ... 12:2) and "*. . . for we have the*
mind of Christ," (1 — nthians 2:16).

Why would I need to renew my mind if I have the mind of Christ? Does Christ's mind need renewing? Of course not! Therefore, these two verses would contradict one another unless there is a difference between your soul and your spirit.

Look further at Ephesians 1:4 that says I am *holy and blameless*, and 2 Peter 1:4 that says I have been made a *partaker of the divine nature*. Yet, I still sin! How can this be? How can I be holy and still sin? Consider this verse, 1 Corinthians 6:17: *"But he who is joined to the Lord becomes one spirit with Him."*

At the moment of saving-faith the Holy Spirit *enters my spirit* bringing with Him the life of Christ, His holy, blameless, righteous, divine life. From that point on, the Lord Jesus and I are *one spirit with each other.* We are not "one *in* spirit" as if to say that He and I, for example, are in agreement on issues. No, He and I are one spirit. My spirit and His life became one spirit. So, inside of me at this moment there are two spirits: the Holy Spirit and my spirit which was re-created by becoming united with the *divine nature* of the Lord Jesus Christ.

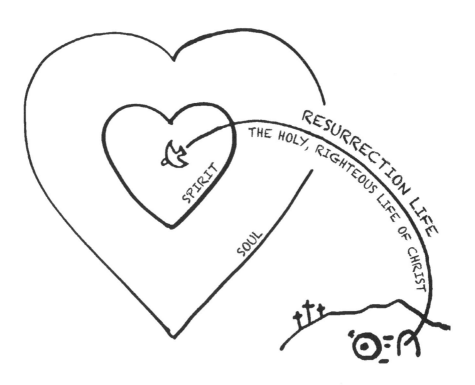

There is a difference between my spirit and my soul. My spirit is one with Christ, and it is holy and blameless, for the divine nature has been imputed into it. But this life, the life of Christ, did not come into the soul. Not at first. I'm going to spend the rest of my life on planet Earth working on renewing my soul, and I will renew it with that same divine life that's in my spirit. The soul is now under new management. A new life in the spirit has come to rule over the soul, and it is the life of the Lord Jesus Christ.

The prayer in Ephesians 3 is very helpful here, too. In this prayer Paul prays that, *"God may grant you to be strengthened with power through His Spirit in your **inner being**. . . ."* The words *inner being* refer to the soul, not the spirit. How do I know this? Take a look at a second time the Apostle Paul used this term. Here is the same Greek phrase in 2 Corinthians 4:16, translated as "inner self:" *"So we do not lose heart. Though our outer self is wasting away, our **inner self** is being renewed day by day."*

In this verse we can see clearly that the "outer self" is referring to the body. After a certain chronological age, our physical bodies begin to waste away. Ecclesiastes 12:3-7 has a fascinating metaphorical description of how age sets in and our bodies break down and decay. But notice the contrast Paul makes. The body is going one way, but the "inner being" or "inner self" is going the opposite direction. It is *being renewed day by day.*

Question. Is that referring to the soul or spirit? It must be the soul. For the spirit is not being renewed day by day. As I would've said as a kid growing up in Texas, "The spirit has done been renewed!" My spirit is not being renewed, for Christ and I are one with each other in the spirit realm. If Christ is not being renewed, then my spirit is not being renewed, either. It has already been renewed. Thus, Paul must be referring to the soul when he speaks of the "inner being" or the "inner self." For, yes, the soul is being renewed day by day as I let the Word of God and the Spirit of God renew it. Clearly, here is another distinction between the spirit and the soul.

The spirit is one with Christ, but the soul is being transformed day by day. If you do not see this, then you will spend your whole life trying to become *Who* you already are. You will spend your time working, striving, whipping up, bucking up, shaping up and trying to get on fire for God (or some other exhortation that the Apostle Paul never used), so that you can become holy and pleasing to Him. When the truth is, He has already made you holy and pleasing to Him—in the spirit. You share His life in your spirit. So you are already holy, righteous, and good in your spirit (not in your soul). For the Holy, Righteous, and Good One of the Universe has shared His life with you.

This is your new identity, and Ephesians 1 has a fuller and more beautiful description of our union with Christ in the spirit. Let's look at what I showed Trooper Girl next.

CHAPTER 12

IDENTITY: The Life in Your Spirit

For in Christ the whole fullness of deity dwells bodily, and you are made full . . .

—Colossians 2:9,10 WEB

Trooper Girl didn't know who she was *in Christ*. I saw that she needed to enter God's rest, beginning with knowing her new identity. She needed to be healed and delivered from her false identity of Daddy's Strong Little Girl, so that she could be her Heavenly Father's little girl, and rest from all her work (Hebrews 4:9,10). She needed to know the new identity in her spirit, who she was *in Christ*. Here's what I showed her.

In Ephesians chapter 1, the Apostle Paul outlines six comforting and encouraging elements about our relationship with God. These elements are intimate blessings that God has granted to us because of His *great kindness*, because of the *riches of His grace*, and because He simply wanted to *lavish* them on us (Ephesians 1:5c,6b,7c,8a,9b). After we hear and believe the simple gospel, that Christ died for our sins and rose again, we can later come to this chapter and discover that our relationship with God has six major blessings. In these He declares our *value* to Him; that we have a new *goodness* in our spirit; and that we have a *power* and *authority* for reigning over our stories. The list starts in verse 4. Here are six blessings of our new *Identity in Christ*.

We were CHOSEN (v. 4). Long before God laid the foundations of the earth, He had compiled a list big enough to be called a book. It was a list of those He wanted for His own possession. You were on the list, if you are a believer in Jesus Christ. That's right, you who are too fat, too slow, too skinny, or too weak; you who were chosen last for every relay race in grade school; you whose ears are too long, and whose thighs are too fat! You were chosen by God. He wanted you. He thinks you're awesome and worthy of love. If you feel unworthy, you hate yourself, you were orphaned by your parents, or you were rejected by the world, God has a new identity for you. The Most Perfect Person in the universe—which, I suppose, would make Him the pickiest Person in the universe—picked you.

That we should be HOLY AND BLAMELESS (v. 4). For us to become His children, God had to share His life with us. Just as your children have your life in them, so also God's children have His life in them. To be born-again, you were reborn with God's very life. He has only one kind of life: eternal, holy, and righteous life. That's the only kind of life He has. In fact, His life is Joyful, Peaceful, Patient, Kind, Good, Faithful, Gentle, and Self-Controlled. Again, that's the only kind of life He has, and He shared it with us. The Holy and Blameless One of the universe imputed His life into us; therefore, we are holy and blameless, too, in our spirit.

In love He . . . ADOPTED us as sons (v. 5). God adopted us. On the surface this might seem less important, for an adopted child might not be regarded as worthy as a natural born child. However, in the culture of the first century, they did not adopt babies. They adopted adults. Historical evidence reveals that in ancient Rome certain people adopted *adults* as a legal maneuver done in the interest of political or economic outcomes. The wealthy ruling class would adopt young men to become ruling heirs, sometimes in place of and in spite of natural born sons who had proven themselves unworthy of ruling. Many of the emperors of Rome came to the throne through adoption. Therefore, in the culture of Rome in the days of the Apostle Paul, adoption was about singling out a person to confer power and authority on him. We were adopted by our Heavenly Father and this grants us power and authority so that we might *reign in life through Jesus Christ* (Romans 5:17).

In Him we have REDEMPTION. By the blood of the Lord Jesus, we were "bought," redeemed out of slavery to sin, and were granted *the FORGIVENESS of our trespasses* (v. 7). God chose me before the foundations of the world, but when He came to get me, he found that I was a slave to sin. But with the death of Jesus a price was paid to buy me out of slavery. Then, knowing that I would come out of that slavery feeling unworthy and ashamed, He pronounced me "Forgiven!" by that same blood of Christ.

Paul's word for "forgiveness" is from the same family of words he used in 1 Corinthians 7:11 for *divorce,* "to put away" your wife. Paul is hinting here in Ephesians 1:7 that we have been *dismissed from,* or *divorced from* our former life of slavery to sin. We are no longer identified with that life. We have been *divorced from our sins,* and are no longer named with them or by them! We have been bought and purchased by a new Lover. Fully Forgiven is our new identity.

In Him . . . we were SEALED with the Holy Spirit (v 13). When we believed and received Jesus Christ, The Holy Spirit came to indwell us as a seal, serving as God's guarantee that we will securely arrive one day at our final destination: His throne room. A seal in the ancient days stood first for a mark of ownership, and that the owner approved of that which he had marked. For us to be sealed with the Holy Spirit means that we have God's sign on us. He owns us and He approves of us, and we are the recipients of the power of heaven.

By these six blessings, it is evident that we are definitely new and improved in the spirit. At the moment of saving-faith, we were completely reconstituted in the spirit (not in the soul; not, yet). We are *chosen, holy and blameless, adopted, redeemed, forgiven, sealed in the Spirit* children of God. When you add Ephesians 2:6, we are already *seated in heaven in Christ Jesus.* Our spirits are united with Christ,

Who lives at the right hand of the Father, so we also have a new address. We are living spiritually in a new locale.

I am . . . a Chosen, Holy & Blameless, Adopted, Redeemed, Forgiven, Sealed with the Holy Spirit, Seated in Heaven, Child of God.

This is the contribution of Ephesians 1 to the study of our new identity in Christ.

Ask most people in church today, "What is your identity?" and they will say, "My identity is who I am." Which actually is to say nothing at all. Of course, your identity is who you are, but *who* are you? Their next reply is, "I am a sinner, saved by grace." To which I reply, "Actually, that phrase is not found in the New Testament." It's found in an old hymnbook, but it's not in the Bible. The more biblical truth would be, I *was* a sinner, but *then* came grace: I was justified freely, born-again with a holy and blameless life, and I have a new identity, a new spirit, in Christ. The Apostle Paul calls us saints. As a saint, I am united with Christ, a possessor of His righteous life, and I am seated at the right hand of the Father (Ephesians 1:22,23; 2:6; Psalm 110:1). This is who we are as believers in Jesus Christ.

In our true life stories we might have been abandoned, neglected, and unwanted; chosen last or rejected altogether. We might have been betrayed by families, lovers, and friends. We might have been unrighteous and blameworthy; aliens to God's household. We've been slaves to sin; needing to be forgiven; with no access to the Spirit of the Father;

separated from Him as unbelievers. In this world we have been labeled as broken, faulty, and told we will never be good enough. We have been discounted, dishonored, even held in contempt. *But God . . .*

But God, being rich in mercy, has brought us into union with Himself through Jesus Christ our Lord. He has made us alive with His resurrection life (Ephesians 2:4). This is our new Identity.

Three Couplets, Four More Blessings

Now, let me show you something else that I notice about this passage. What if we coupled these six blessings into three different sets? Like this:

CHOSEN
REDEEMED

HOLY and BLAMELESS
FORGIVEN

ADOPTED
SEALED IN THE SPIRIT

One day while studying this passage I noticed there could be a relationship between *CHOSEN* and *REDEEMED*. It seemed in my mind that these two words spoke of our VALUE to God. I am so valuable to God that He still wanted me, even after He knew my whole life of sins that I would choose. He still wanted me! He would still redeem me from my slavery to sin. I am valuable to Him.

I then noticed that *ADOPTED* and *SEALED WITH THE SPIRIT* also appeared related. These two, based on the history of that culture, speak of our AUTHORITY and POWER, respectively, in Christ.

After those two couplings, I was left with *HOLY and BLAMELESS* and *FORGIVEN*. I was not sure how these two concepts related, until I was recently struck with an observation I made from a story in our national news: there is a common desire among human beings to be regarded as "a good person." Most people, religious or not, want their epitaph to read, *"She was a good person."* We are a planet full of people wanting to be known as good and decent human beings, and we've wanted it since we ate from that tree in the Garden. Before we came to Christ none of us were righteous, but we could *act* good, and we could strive to earn a fine eulogy at our funeral service.

However, the believer today *is* good. There is a place inside of us that is good. It's in our spirit where we have a new heart. It is not a goodness of our own, but the goodness of the *holy and blameless life of a forgiven child of God.* There is a place inside of us, a place called spirit, where we are one with Christ, and we are good and godly there. The Holy and Blameless One of the universe has shared His life with us, and His moral goodness is now our life. The Eternal Forgiver of the Universe has shared His life with us, so His forgiving life is now our life. By nature we are good. By nature we are forgivers, too! His **goodness** is our life. This is our identity in the spirit.

Thus, your spirit is fine. It is perfectly fine, for it is one with Christ (1 Corinthians 6:17). Feeling unloved and unwanted today? That feeling is not in your spirit, for a holy God has chosen you and wants you. Are you feeling ashamed and condemned today? Those labels are not in your spirit, for there is no condemnation to those who are holy and blameless in Christ Jesus. Are you discouraged? Defeated? Hopeless and afraid? *It can't be in your spirit!* For Jesus is not discouraged, defeated, hopeless, or afraid. All of those negative emotions and thoughts are in your soul! It's your shame and the manifestation of your Shame-based identity. *That* identity, an identity built around shame, is in your soul.

Let this Scripture cancel out that old identity. Leave that old identity, and don't let it reign over you. Let's walk through this passage again, and consider what God has done to make you new *in the spirit*, the place of your nature, your essence, your identity.

God *chose* you before He ever created you, when you were only in His holy imagination. Then sometime in these modern times, He came to get you for Himself. His angels pointed out the sinful mess you were in, but the Father said, "I'm in the **redemption** business, so you angels get him to the church on time."

However, you alleged, "But God, you don't know who I am." He replied, "Yes, I do. You're a sinner, but now I am going to make you a saint. I'm going to give you My life, My *Holy and Blameless* Life and change who you are."

Then you mumbled, "But God, you don't know what I've done." He replied, "I know exactly what you have done, but I hereby grant you a divorce from your sins, and I have *forgiven* all of it, just as I am forgetting it."

Then you said, "But God, I'm not worthy of your kingdom, just let me live in the barn and feed the pigs." But God beamed, "I have *adopted* you, now. You are coming to My home to reign and rule in kingdom business with Me."

Finally you lamented, "But God, I have no power for such a privileged position." He replied, "You do now, for I am *sealing* you as My own possession with the Holy Spirit now living in you. He will teach you how to walk in My power and authority. Come *sit at my right hand*, united with Christ, and reign with us."

To deliver us from *who* we once were, God has granted us the intimacy and privilege of a new identity. We have been brought into a relationship that reconstituted our spirit. He determined it. He intended it. He accomplished it. He granted it. He delighted in it.

But there's one more important thing to know in this passage. How does God establish us to stand in this identity?

CHAPTER 13

How God Teaches Us Our Identity

When the Holy Spirit opens the eyes of your heart to see, you won't need to take notes.

E rin's eyes filled with tears as we talked. Her heart filled with peace and relief as we walked through Ephesians 1. She had never studied this chapter, and my simple outline and explanation gave her sweet comfort as it connected with her spirit. I drew a sheet of paper for Trooper Girl Erin, and it looked like this:

IDENTITY	
CHOSEN REDEEMED	VALUE
HOLY and BLAMELESS FORGIVEN	GOODNESS
ADOPTED SEALED with HOLY SPIRIT	POWER and AUTHORITY

"But why don't I live in this? Why can't I live in this?" she asked. Then I began to expand on my paper outline. Silently, I wrote the right-hand column (below) as Erin watched.

IDENTITY		
CHOSEN REDEEMED	VALUE	EMOTIONALLY ABUSED COVERTLY REJECTED "I DON'T MATTER" WORTHLESS
HOLY and BLAMELESS FORGIVEN	GOODNESS	BE PERFECT and GOOD BE THERE FOR OTHERS DON'T BE NEEDY BE A DOORMAT PEOPLE-PLEASER
ADOPTED SEALED/HOLY SPIRIT	POWER and AUTHORITY	UNHEALED WEAK, FRAGILE STRONG IN THE FLESH

As I began to write out the column on the right side of the paper, tears ran down Erin's cheeks. She began to see the shame-based identity that gripped her heart. The false self of "Trooper Girl" was actually a front. A fraud. It was merely a cover-up for the shame that controlled the conversations in her head. Erin realized that her divorcing-dad had been emotionally insensitive to her. What a coward! He made Erin announce his departure and divorce plans. That wasn't her job! She acquiesced to his abuse by accepting his marching orders.

She began to weep as I told her that this was a form of rejection. That her dad was telling her that she didn't matter. Her emotions and desires were not important at that time. His were. The important thing was for him to get his blasted coffee cup and get out of the house before Mom came home! He must take care of himself, and leave Erin to hold up the collapsing family situation. For him, Erin's personal shock and upset were not important. In fact, perhaps his coffee cup was more important than she.

This was a form of rejection.

The truth settled in her. Her dad was actually telling her that she had little *value*, except in how she could serve his cowardice.

Then her mother checked out, too. She checked out emotionally. This left Erin as an emotional orphan, for now she had "lost" both of her parents.

Then sober disappointment gathered in her heart as she looked at her phony sense of *goodness*. By trying to be ever-present for others, denying her own emotional pain and her own intimacy needs, Erin was a caretaker to a fault. It is a godly thing to look after your own family, but it is not godly to neglect the care of your own heart. There is a healthy principle recognized by the airline industry: "If the cabin should lose pressure an oxygen mask will drop down from above you. If you are traveling with children or the elderly, place your mask on first; then assist those who need help." *Take care of yourself, so you can take care of others.*

Erin had not been taking care of her heart. She was not "guarding her heart" (Proverbs 4:23). She wasn't loving her neighbor well, for she was not loving herself well (Matthew 22:39). She had spent years ignoring her own needs, being dutiful to take care of others, even to the point of being a doormat who let others use her for their own care. Even after her husband physically manhandled her—on three occasions!—Erin did not bring down on him the kind of consequences that would force him to get help. Others were more important, in a sick and unhealthy way.

Third, she had no *power and authority* to stand up to this situation and exhort her family to get healthy. She didn't do it for herself. She stood strong in the flesh of Trooper Girl, and could not allow herself to be devastated by her dad's departure. Her strength was of the flesh, not of the Spirit. She considered it godly to be strong in herself. Now she was quite weak and broken from the lack of healing and comfort that God and other godly women could have provided.

Trooper Girl was the false self of a woman who was undervalued and diminished of worthiness by her parents. These two weak people had been using their firstborn child to be their moral and spiritual leader: *"She can be the officer on duty, while we grown-ups skip out and drop out."* Many parents skate on being the leader, and demand more of their children than they are willing to demand of themselves.

Erin was grateful to read in Ephesians of her new identity. She would have liked very much to get out of the shame-based identity and grow in the love and acceptance of her new identity in Christ.

But how?

How do you get out of the old identity and into the new identity? How do you make a change at the level of identity?

I told her that the key for making that change was in this same passage. Look at Ephesians 1:16-18. After telling the Ephesians that they are chosen, holy and blameless, adopted, redeemed, forgiven, sealed in the Spirit, children of God, then he prays. Paul stops his Bible study to tell the Ephesians that he is going to pray for them now. What is he going to pray?

Paul prays for two important revelations. In verse 17 he prays that God *will give them a spirit of wisdom and revelation into the true knowledge of Him.* When you get a revelation of who God is, then at the same time you get a revelation of who you are. Intimacy with God always leads to intimacy with yourself. When you see the glory of the holiness of God, then your own fleshly ways will be exposed in that light. What Erin needed first was for God to reveal to her when she was walking in the shame-based identity. When the conversations of her mind were ruminating with self-deprecating messages of, *"I am worthless; I am not important; I don't matter; others deserve but I don't; I'm a reject,"* then Erin needed the Holy Spirit to call this to her attention and reveal it to her.

When Erin's mind began to tell her that she needed to *be perfect for others, that she couldn't be needy, she must be strong, that others needed her to be strong so they could be happy,* then Erin was walking according to the flesh. Her shame was kicking in, and she was protecting herself, or providing for herself, by being everyone's perfect helper. So, second, she needed the Holy Spirit to reveal to her that other people were wiping their feet on her. The Spirit must reveal to Erin what she was thinking and how she was acting.

Third, Erin needed the Holy Spirit to break through to her about her fleshly sense of power, that her false self was working too hard to prop herself up to look powerful and present for everyone else. The truth was, when walking in her unhealed shame, Erin was weak and fragile. Her mind set on the flesh is telling her that she needs to be stronger for her family; that the good Christian mother must take care of others but never take care of herself. This fleshly sense of power was actually killing her instead of helping her. She needed the Holy Spirit to gently call her on it.

Thus, Paul's prayer in Ephesians 1:17 is for the Holy Spirit to reveal to our spirit that we are walking in our shame-based identity; to reveal that we are walking in the twisted sense of the value, goodness, and power that we developed on our own, as we sought to protect or provide for ourselves in response to our shame.

Next, Paul prays in verse 18 that *the Holy Spirit would open the eyes of our heart "to see" the hope of our calling.* What is the hope of our calling? In the context of Ephesians chapter 1, this hope is our new identity *in Christ,* that we are chosen, holy and blameless, adopted, redeemed, forgiven, sealed in the Spirit, children of God. This is our hope: Christ for us, and in us, with a new identity. Our calling is to enter into the reality of this new intimacy with Christ, and to rest in the value, goodness, and power of this blessed relationship.

The "eyes of our heart" need to be opened to "see" this hope, to "see" the value of the spiritual blessings of our intimate relationship with God. But we cannot see it, in a transforming way, until the Holy Spirit opens the eyes of our heart. That is to say, *this new identity is Spirit-taught*. The Holy Spirit "teaches" it to us. You do not get it on your own. Your pastor does not teach it to you. He may preach about it, explain the passage to you, diagram or illustrate it, but you do not get it merely because you read it with the eyes of your head. The eyes of your heart have to see it. Every passage in the New Testament about our identity is taught to us personally and privately by the Holy Spirit. If He does not teach us, it will remain as mere words on the page. Paul is praying in verse 18 that the Holy Spirit will open the eyes of our heart and reveal to us our value, goodness, and power as it is identified in 1:3-14.

We do not need to be taught our shame-based identity (on the right side of Erin's paper). We already know that. We taught it to ourselves growing up! We now need for the Holy Spirit to simply reveal to us when we are walking in it.

But we do need to be taught our new identity in Christ (on the left side of Erin's paper). Therefore, when the Holy Spirit reveals to Erin that she is walking in rejection and worthlessness, no more valuable than a coffee cup, He can then speak to her of her value to Father. She was chosen and redeemed; she was bought with a price. Her Heavenly Father has not rejected her. He has declared her value and worth.

When the Holy Spirit catches Erin walking as a people-pleasing doormat, being there for others but with her heart full of resentment and anger about it, then He can reveal to her that she is walking in her own goodness—a phony, frustrating goodness that only leaves her more empty and angry. One of the definitions of co-dependency is this: trying to heal something broken inside of you by serving and giving to another person in the hope that you will be fixed by this other person not just loving you back, but *needing* you; and that this neediness for you will somehow fix you, heal you.

When Erin walks in her fleshly version of co-dependency, then the Holy Spirit can first open the eyes of her heart to "see" that in her spirit she has already been fixed. God fixed her with a new identity. She doesn't need others to fix her. The Lord chose her, paid a precious price for her, and shared His life with her. He fixed her. He fixed her with the gift of His life (Romans 5:17b, 19b; Colossians 3:4), and now she is holy and blameless. She doesn't need to be a doormat, a phony lover of others, in an attempt to be perceived as "good." She is good in the spirit (not in her flesh!), with a goodness she received from Christ. She can serve and love others with His life as her goodness. She can allow the Holy Spirit to interrupt her flesh-walk and reveal her true goodness in Christ, then lead her to walk in the Spirit.

When Erin loses her voice, and doesn't speak up for herself; when she gets overwhelmed and feels weak, powerless, and unhealed, then she must not choose to be strong in the strength of her own soul, as Trooper Girl. Instead, she can admit her weakness, admit her powerlessness, and then present herself to the Spirit of life in Christ Jesus (Romans 8:2) to lift her to a new stamina that is from Christ, her life. In Christ she has a voice. In Christ she has power. In fact, in Christ's power she can even say "No" to dependent people who need to trust God rather than be trusting Erin.

How do you make a change at the level of Identity? How do you get out of your shame-based identity and into your grace-based identity in Christ? It starts by getting on your knees to pray, with the Bible in front of you opened to Ephesians 1. Pray through this chapter and pray Paul's prayer for yourself. Ask God to open your ears to "hear" His voice when He reveals to you that you are living in your false self. Ask God to enlighten the eyes of your heart to know your new identity in Christ. Then ask Him which blessing (chosen? adopted? forgiven?) is pertinent to your trial or situation. Ask Him to "teach" you how this blessing is your hope and calling.

When the Holy Spirit opens the eyes of your heart to "see" something of this blessed new identity, you will not need to take notes. You will get it. You will get it in the deep places of your soul. Then Christ will dwell in that new place (Ephesians 3:17). Your mind will be opened to a level of renewal you have never known before. Your soul will begin to open to a Spirit-led transformation, as your old immune system, inoculated against change, will begin to break down. Your will-to-resist will bow before a new vision, a new sense that, "I not only must change and live in this new identity, but I can change, I can live in it. In fact, I will change; I cannot *not* change."

You will be making a change at the level of identity, and you will be learning something about grace that usually only the desperate, recovering addict learns. We learn the best when we are desperate. That desperation comes from the damage in the soul. Our spirit is fine, but our soul is not. Let's look at how our shame-based identity developed from the damage in the soul.

CHAPTER 14

Your Damage in the Soul: The Emergence of Shame

"It's not good for man to be alone."

—God

K atherine came to counsel with me complaining about her two married sons. Now that she was a widow, her grown sons and their families never spent enough time with her. I thought I detected the sound of a victim in her voice. As we got into Katherine's story, however, I discovered that she truly was a victim, in a way. It started even before she was born. Here's her story.

Katherine was to be born the third child in her family, and be greeted into the world by an older sister, Betsy, and a brother, Bill. Tragically, two weeks before Katherine was born, in a routine tonsillectomy on Betsy, inexplicably and shockingly, six year-old Betsy died in the recovery room!

Oh, the grief that struck her parents, a grief from which they never seemed to recover. Medical research today has argued that the emotional state of the mother can affect the unborn child, especially in the later months of the pregnancy. Can you imagine the sudden deluge and baptism of grief, despair, and depression that was felt by Katherine in the womb?

Less than two weeks after Betsy's funeral, Katherine was born. She came into a home that was in deep anguish, to a depressed and broken-hearted mother and father. Unable to heal from their grief, Katherine's parents failed to emotionally attach to her, and she felt like an orphan in her own home. Where there should have been joy, there was aloneness.

As she grew old enough to learn of her sister's death, Katherine continued on through childhood and beyond with this identity: *"I am an unacceptable replacement for a beloved, lost child."*

Her parents' sadness ruled their home, and Katherine even felt detached from her older brother. It seemed to her that he treated Katherine as if she were a pesky neighbor-child from next-door, instead of as his precious little sister. Her younger years were built around the false identity she developed in her heart as an "orphan-child." As she grew, she was overly sensitive to all of life's hurts or rejections. Katherine grew weak from the damaging belief in her heart that she was a discounted, unacceptable replacement child.

"It is not good for man to be alone." We are wired by God for loving, connecting, and belonging; however, instead of intimacy, *aloneness* happens. In Katherine's story we see three of the four major kinds of damage that happen in the soul. *Aloneness* comes to reside in our souls through *holes, wounds, arrows, and fault-lines.*

Holes

A *Hole* is when we don't get what we *should* get. That is, we are born for intimacy, but in many families it can be so scarce. As a result, we might miss out on love, acceptance, and affirmation, and end up with a hole, an emptiness, in our soul. A hole can also come from relational and emotional neglect or abandonment. In Katherine's story, she had a hole in her soul as she did not get cuddled and kissed, cherished and delighted over. She did not get what babies need! She never got what little girls need. A huge hole began emerging in her soul from the very first day she came home from the hospital as a newborn.

You might say, "Well, her story is not mine; her story is a little over the top." I agree that Katherine "over-illustrates" the point. However, most everyone that I counsel with readily acknowledges that while growing up love was scarcer than they had wished.

Wounds

Second, alongside a hole, we might get something more painful, a *Wound*. A wound is where we *do* get what we *shouldn't* get. Thankfully, this didn't also happen to Katherine, but for many others of us it did. Wounds are when we get slapped, punched, yanked, or hit by a parent. Wounds happen when we get emotionally scarred from a parent screaming and raging in our face; we are overly punished for a much milder offense; we get humiliated and scolded for simply being afraid; we get spanked more for crying; we get molested by a sibling or other relative; or we get bullied at school; ridiculed by our friends; humiliated in front of the class; get chosen last; or not chosen at all. Harsh and hurtful words and actions leave wounds that reside in our soul. Let"s draw a wound like this:

Arrows

The third manner in which Aloneness comes to haunt our soul is when we are rejected. We take *Arrows* of pain and hurt when betrayed and abandoned by loved ones and friends.

Now, of course, a rejection is a kind of wound; however, rejections are so much more painful and personal that I think they deserve a category of their own. Rejections are emotionally debilitating because the person who afflicted us was someone who had promised to love us, promised to be there for us. At least, this person should've known better. Thus, we have more pain from rejections. We cry more when rejected.

Remember in the fifth grade, women? Remember when you and your girlfriends were all sweet friends at morning recess, and plans were made on Tuesday for a Friday night sleepover at one of their homes? But something happened on Wednesday when somebody said something hurtful. Then somebody said something else. Now there's a misunderstanding. By afternoon recess you were out! One of the girls was mad at you, and you were no longer invited to the slumber party. Your mother was not called and given the invitation. You were not included. Left out. You spent Friday night at home alone. Your mother was at her sewing counter with her back to you, and your dad was watching his shows on TV. You were *alone* and painfully aware that the other girls were having fun. Rejection. Pain. *Aloneness*.

We men remember very clearly the first girl that rejected us. In the fifth grade I was in love with Joanne, and hoping that she would find me cute. She didn't. Rejection. The next year, I thought, I will show her. I'll get Lisa to go with me, and Joanne will be jealous. Lisa agreed for a little while, but then she broke up with me. More rejection. More pain. That story often repeats itself a few more times in life.

Many teenage boys and girls are walking around the halls of high school with these invisible arrows sticking out of their souls. Many adults are walking around the church with the invisible arrows of divorce stuck in their souls.

Fault Lines

All the while that we are getting holes, wounds, and rejection arrows in our souls, something else is happening in the soul. Fault lines are cracking down the wall of the soul. When we are wounded, hurt, and rejected, we lie in bed at night and relive the memory. We go over the memory again and again, and as we tell ourselves the "truth" of what happened, something begins to emerge in our mind: fault lines. We start to tell ourselves that we are faulty. We silently tell ourselves that it was our fault and that something's wrong with us. Can you imagine how often Katherine would lie in bed and wonder about the meaning of this emptiness she felt every day?

For others, consider when a parent regularly screams and yells at a child. Little children ages three, four, or five do not have the emotional and mental capacity to say, "Gee, Dad sure is mad, I guess he had a bad day at work." No, little children think with immature development. Unable to individuate from their parents, children think, "If Dad is mad, then I am bad. I can't do anything right; I always make my daddy angry; there must be something wrong with me; I'm faulty." Children easily develop a false sense of faultiness about themselves. As Dad rages throughout the years, a child spends three to five years (or longer) thinking like this. These faulty ways of thinking get entrenched in the heart: "I'm bad; I can't do anything right; I'm not worth it; I can't make anybody happy; maybe I shouldn't have even been born."

When we feel the empty *holes* in our soul, we tell ourselves that we are unloved and unwanted because something is wrong with us.

When we ache over the painful *wounds* in our soul, we take it to mean that we are bad, stupid, or broken and damaged.

When we are rejected by those we love, when we feel those *arrows* piercing our soul, we tell ourselves that we are not acceptable, not worthy enough; or that we will never be happy; or that we will never be loved the way we want to be loved. We tell ourselves there's something wrong with us; that we are rejects; that there is something faulty about us.

Fault lines in the soul look like this:

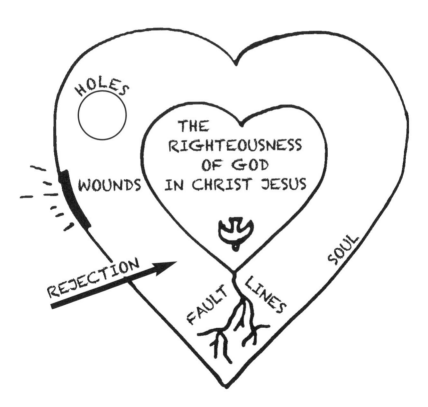

Life is painful. Life in Adam can be excruciatingly painful. All of us have holes, wounds, and arrows that have hurt us. This pain contributes to our development of a diminishing identity. Hurtful experiences have a way of "telling" us that we are unloved, unacceptable, unforgivable, or unworthy. The gradual build-up in the heart of these unresolved hurts can lead us to lower our opinion of our personal worth and goodness (identity). This then becomes our Shame-based Identity.

Let's outline again the difference between the shame-based identity and the false self, i.e., between the truly *alone* person and the poser.

First, out of the holes, wounds, and arrows in my life, I develop a diminishing view of myself. This view of myself is represented by a conversation playing in my head. Second, these "sentences" of the conversation are the fault lines, the lies around which I accept this Shame-based Identity.

Third, out of this Shame-based Identity I must now find ways to cope. I must find a strategy to survive living in this shame. Therefore, I seek out ways to protect, provide for, promote, or pleasure myself. Feeling "naked and ashamed," I develop my unique, negative flesh patterns: drinking, drugging, sexing, lying, hiding, hurting, judging, criticizing, and other ways of controlling.

Fourth, I now need to hide or minimize these negative flesh-patterns and make sure no one ever knows how inadequate I feel about myself. So, I develop positive flesh-patterns that become the behaviors of my False Self. The False Self covers up what's really going on inside. It covers up the fact that I actually am deeply ashamed of or frustrated with who I am. The False Self emerges as a polished, posturing poser. A phony. To hide my Shame-based Identity (the true story of my holes, wounds, and rejections), I develop this imposter who bluffs his way through life—always talking, always laughing, always bragging. Posing as if I am somebody I am not. The False Self is a fraud. The False Self is not authentic.

The False Self goes to church. The False Self can smile while handing out the church bulletin. She can teach the adult women's class. She can sing a solo at the offertory. He can preach a sermon, and a good one, too. The False Self props himself up behind many roles, while hiding, bluffing, posing, posturing, smiling, pleasing, serving, preaching, singing, faking it, half-making it, and all the while hoping that you don't see his imperfections.

The False Self can spend a lot of energy in what we call *Image Management*: trying to project outwardly a sense of control, to keep others from seeing the pain and mismanagement on the inside.

> **Image Management:**
>
> Purposefully, over-representing yourself professionally, socially, spiritually and/or intellectually to mask your imperfections.

Addicts never can hide quite so well. We mismanage our time and our money. We mismanage our relationships; we break promises and disappoint; we break more promises and create more pain; we fall from the places we hide; we bluff and pose until we look ridiculous; we posture but collapse in our own lack of credibility. We can fake it for a while; and we can even half-make it, for a while. Eventually, our imperfections become too obvious.

The rest of you in the church do a much better job of hiding, because your compulsions are not as offensive. But we all need grace and its wonder-working power. We addicts invite the rest of you in the church to join us in coming out of hiding. Quit being so perfect! Image management is too stressful. Come find Grace. One of the best places to start unraveling this puzzle is found when you analyze your Emotional Cup.

CHAPTER 15

Your Emotional Cup: The Starting Place for Healing

"Even a minor event in the life of a child is an event of that child's world and thus a world event."

—Gaston Bachelard

God designed us for His world. His world is one of love, joy, peace, patience, kindness, goodness, and gentleness. Pain was not a part of nature as He created it. We were not created for pain and shame. This is why we are not skilled at absorbing and dealing with hurts, upsets, rejections, and pain. We don't know how to get rid of pain. We tend to get stuck in our pain. Dr. Brene Brown said in her original TED Talk,[4]

---

[4] Brown, B. (2010, June). *Brene Brown: The Power of Vulnerability* [Video file]. Retrieved from https://www.ted.com/talks/brene_brown _on_vulnerability#t-82744

"When you ask people about love, they tell you about heartbreak;
when you ask people about belonging,
they tell you excruciating stories about being excluded;
and when you ask people about connection,
they tell stories about disconnection."

When we tell our stories of pain, we speak from hearts that are unhealed. However, there is something in the universe that can heal pain. We just don't get much of it. It's called intimacy. We are wired by God for intimacy. We are wired for intimacy with Him, with ourselves,[5] and with others; but, again, we don't seem to get much of it.

We respond to, and grow best in, an environment where there is Love, Acceptance, Affirmation, Nurture, Forgiveness, Mercy, Grace, Boundaries, and Guidance (to name a few). These quality gifts are the ingredients for healthy intimacy. We grow as humans when as children we receive these from our parents. We grow when we give them to one another. They are the gifts of unconditional love.

We learned in elementary school that a plant grows if you provide it with nutritious soil, adequate sunshine, and adequate water. So also in the same way, human beings

---

[5] Intimacy with ourselves is not something sinister. I am referring to having an awareness of yourself, being aware of your life story, your hurts, your thoughts, your own flesh patterns; being aware of what "triggers" your selfish behavior. Without this self-awareness, this intimacy with yourself, you will never break stronghold patterns in your life, and you might never have intimacy with others.

grow and heal, emotionally and relationally, if you provide an environment of love and acceptance; with affection and affirmation; with mercy and forgiveness for their mistakes; with grace to encourage a despondent heart; with healthy boundaries to teach respect; and with guidance to grant wisdom in the teaching-moments along life's journey. These are some of the ingredients of intimacy and bonding love. If we provide these things—like nutritious soil, sunshine, and water for a plant—humans will respond and grow into "persons," healthier people who love, connect, and bond with others. Intimacy is the greatest healing and nurturing tool in the universe.

Instead of intimacy, however, aloneness happens. Instead of intimacy, pain happens, and it becomes the seeding ground for addictions and compulsions. We can see what this does in our hearts when we look into our emotional cups.

Imagine, if you will, that your emotions are contained in a large cup inside your spirit-soul dimension. We only have a limited emotional capacity, just as every cup only holds a limited amount. If you were holding a 26 oz. cup in your hands, and I were filling it up with water, where would the twenty-seventh ounce of water go if I were not paying attention? It would spill out of the cup, onto the floor, splashing on the shoes and socks of anyone nearby. Our emotions are the same. We only have a capacity for a limited amount, and once my cup is full, then any more emotions will spill out and onto others, or as we might say, "I will take it out on others."

Our emotional cup first begins to fill up with emotional Pain and Hurt.

"ALONENESS "

FEAR

ANGER

PAIN

Our childhood *pain* can come from anywhere. Your parents fight and then divorce; your parents fight and don't divorce; your mother in various ways tells you that you're not pretty enough; your grandmother favors your sibling over you; your father is filled with rage and beats you, yanks you, pulls you up by your hair; he lies to cover his own sin and tells you there is something mentally wrong with you to accuse him; you are close to your grandfather and he dies; your sibling gets a rare disease and dies; your best friend in elementary school is killed in a car wreck; you move to a new town and you're the new kid, again; you are humiliated at school for being too dumb, too short, too skinny, too ugly or too fat, and you wish that you could die.

Pain can come in a myriad of ways, and childhood pain seems to stay in the bottom of the heart. The word "pain" is a blanket term for all kinds of emotional hurt, such as feeling insecure, fearful, worthless, unloved, unwanted, damaged, wounded, rejected, abused, etc. If we do not process[6] this pain and hurt in a healthy manner, then something else automatically emerges in our emotional cup.

How do we like Pain? We don't. It makes us mad. *Anger* automatically flows from our pain. It can come from other people's sins against us, and so we are angry with those people. Our pain can come from our own mistakes and humiliations, and so we are angry with ourselves. Our pain can come from the providential events of life, and so we can be angry with God. Pain always grows into anger, for we are mad that life has hurt us. When you meet an angry person, you can bank on it, that this is someone with a lot of hurt and pain in his heart.

If a person never deals with this pain and anger, if he never reduces it by telling the story to Mother and Father, or never talks it out in prayer with God or other intimate friends, then something else begins to emerge in his emotional cup.

---

[6] "Process" is a favorite word of counselors, isn't it? Actually, it is a good word. It is from the Latin, "to proceed, to go forward." We use this term to speak of handling and organizing our thoughts around a painful event by means of talking about it with someone, even praying about it with God, so as to clarify and discern what really happened; so as to reject any lies or misunderstandings; so as to seek comfort from the pain; so as to put away anger; so as to accept and make amends as necessary; so as to live in the truth; so as to proceed, go forward, and "get over it." See, it's a great word!

If you never deal with the Pain and the Anger, then the *fear* that has been lurking around from the beginning of the pain will begin to form its own stronghold in your soul. It is the Fear that the Pain will never stop; Fear that the Pain will never go away; or the Fear that those creating the Pain will not quit; or that you will get a worse spanking if you speak up; or the Fear that your life will always be this Pain and Anger, Pain and Anger, Pain and Anger; or even the Fear that you will hurt someone with your Anger.

This Fear is the automatic emotional response to unresolved Pain and Anger, and it immobilizes you. Fear causes you to run and hide. It produces anxiety, worry, panic and control. Fear causes you to criticize and judge others; or it can move you in the opposite direction to play the nice guy and be passive. Fear can drive you to be controlling and manipulative. Control freaks are people controlled by fear.

People full of Pain, Anger, and Fear are people full of conflict: mental, emotional, and spiritual conflict. These, of course, all lead to relational conflict. People carrying around this kind of inner conflict have trouble with relationships. You cannot have a soul full of anger and not have it affect your closest relationships. Thus, the next layer in the Emotional Cup is *"Aloneness."*

"Aloneness" is in quotation marks because it's the word from Genesis 2, where God said, "It is not good for the man to be alone." Adam was with God the Father, Son, and Holy Spirit every day, so he was not lonely, but he was alone. Even with the Triune God in his life, it was God who said that Adam was alone.

The Father did not say, "Tell you what, Adam, since you are alone, our solution is to split up; the Son and the Holy Spirit and I will each come separately down to the Garden during the day and We will split our time with you; then you will have One of us here walking with you in the Garden three times a day."

No, the solution to Adam's aloneness was not to have more of God. The solution to aloneness was another human being. Keep that in mind the next time you are alone and hurting, and you wonder where God is. He is coming to you through those friends He keeps sending to you, those friends you keep resisting and pushing away or hiding from, whenever they try to get near to comfort you.

Then sin enters the picture in Genesis 3, and along with sin comes the breaking apart of relationships. God comes down to the Garden and tells Adam and Eve of the impending changes. Can you imagine with me? God approaches in the Garden of Eden and tells Adam and Eve to pack their bags, for they will be leaving the Garden first thing in the morning. After God leaves can you imagine that Adam turns and stomps off to the other side of the garden, leaving Eve standing there alone? He is in one corner of the Garden frustrated, kicking dirt clods, mad at himself, mad at Eve, and mad that everything now has been ruined. Then I can imagine that Eve is in the other corner of the Garden. She's weeping and worrying that Adam will never speak to her again; that he's mad as a hornet (or a bee or a wasp, or whatever that flying thing was that he told her the other day to watch out for); that he's going to break off their relationship, divorce her, go back to his comfortable life as a bachelor, and that she's ruined everything for good!

In Genesis 2 Adam was alone, but he didn't even know it. However, at the end of chapter 3, he is alone and he knows it. In fact, from Genesis 3 until today, Man continues to suffer from broken relationships. We are "alone" and we know it! Today, our Pain, Anger, and Fear alienate us from one another, and we know we are "alone."

Aloneness is the dreadful emotion one feels when there is a lack of healthy intimacy in one's life. It is the emotional and mental state when one acknowledges a lack of love, acceptance, nurturing, encouragement, forgiveness and mercy. Aloneness is painful.

We go to family gatherings for Thanksgiving dinner, and the same old arguments and attitudes arrive before the pumpkin pie, and we are "alone" and we know it, in a room full of family members.

You feel this "aloneness" when you and your spouse have the same old argument because you have never resolved your differences on some matter, and once again there is conflict over it. You lie awake in bed that night with your backs to each other. You are "alone" and you know it.

I counseled with Jim for several months about the pain he felt as a young adolescent in his home with unloving parents. As a young adolescent he would go to church with his parents on Sundays, scan the crowded pews and say to himself, "My *real* parents are somewhere here in the church, and after the service today they are going to come and get me and take me home with them, and I will at last be loved and accepted, and live happily ever after." Jim sat in a crowded church service, in the same pew with his actual parents and siblings, but he was "alone" and he knew it.

We experience the Garden of Eden "Aloneness" in our lives today, and we also agree with God: *it is not good for man to be alone.* It's so painful. What do we do with our Aloneness?

We seek comfort.

Everyone seeks comfort to feel better. We don't enjoy feeling pain, anger, and fear. We don't enjoy the emptiness and loneliness that comes from relationships that are damaged by these toxic emotions, so we seek comfort. Consider the list below of some of the ways we seek comfort.

Seek Comfort

"ALONENESS"

FEAR

ANGER

PAIN

Drinking
Drugs
Overeating
Pornography
Sexual Behaviors
Computer Games
Academics
Sports
Shopping
Religion
Perfectionism
Adrenaline Rushes

When our cup is filled with these negative emotions we feel disconnected. In this pain we seek comfort. This is how, as young people, we get dependent on drinking heavily with our friends, or we start experimenting with drugs. In loneliness we might be sexually active in an attempt to "find love." Others of us get lost in video games and withdraw from socializing. We can get lost and alone while isolating ourselves to make straight A's in school; we can hide—and take out—our frustration and anger in sports. Women go shopping, alone. Men go fishing, alone. Some people get too religious (Ecclesiastes 7:16), and end up alone at church. Others get advanced degrees in perfectionism! We live in extremes, looking for a rush of adrenalin. We do all this when we feel "aloneness."

We are seeking comfort.

In our pursuit to feel better we can get addicted to these behaviors because our need to feel better is so great. Years later in life we realize that we are destroying our ability to relate to our spouse and children because these behaviors have taken over our lives.

Then we might ask God for help.

Here begins the new problem. We want God to deliver us from one of these destructive behaviors, so we start praying for Him to get us out. We cry for Him to deliver us from this hurtful behavior. Our spouse threatens to leave us if we don't fix this problem. We get desperate. We pray harder to be delivered. We join a men's group at church to try to fix it. We let our spouse put us under new rules and regulations of the things we must now do to show her that we are "working on it." Wives become policemen and husbands feel like little boys. Nothing good happens out of that.

We are frustrated. We are enslaved. The more we focus on the sin, the more it seems to defeat us. In fact, Romans 7:13 tells us that if we put ourselves under new rules and regulations to try to quit sinning, the opposite will happen. Our sin will grow. Our sin will grow stronger. Our sin will become utterly sinful!

I counsel with men all the time who do this with their pornography addiction. They pray for God to take it away. They grow desperate when it doesn't happen. They pray harder. They pray some more. They fail, again. They look, again. They prove that they are addicted. They get angry. They get sorrowful. They try again. They then get mad at God and me and say that counseling is not helping. In exasperation they say, "What good is God?"

What's the problem? God is ready to help them. He wants to deliver them. It's just that His way of deliverance is not evident to them until I draw this emotional cup diagram. Follow me closely here.

Where is "pornography" on this diagram?

It's in the right hand column. It's in the list of ways to seek comfort. Porn is an attempt to get comfort. It's a failing attempt to solve a problem. What's the *real* problem? The real problem is the pain, anger, fear, and aloneness. The pornography is not *the* problem. *The* problem is that I feel so terrible in my heart. The painful emotions in the cup are driving the compulsion to look at porn in an attempt to find comfort.

The men who can't quit are the men who, in their agony, drop to their knees in the right hand column. They drop to their knees *in their sin*, and beg God to come over to the place of their sin and deliver them from the sin. But that's not where God is! Quit standing in your "comfort-seeking sins" asking God to deliver you *from there*! He doesn't meet you there.

Where does God want to meet you?

He's standing over in the bottom of your emotional cup. He's standing over there inviting you to join Him in addressing the real problem: your pain!

Are you struggling with a judgmental, critical spirit? It's coming from your pain. Somebody hurt you and you are angry.

Are you bound up in unforgiveness? It's coming from your pain. You struggle to forgive the person who offended you because you need more healing.

Are you overeating, drinking too much, or spending compulsively? It's coming from your pain. Heal your pain first. You are failing to find comfort in those compulsive behaviors, because your pain is unhealed.

When Christians finally discover the healing grace of God, they discover it at the bottom of their emotional cup. That's where God wants to meet you. From the bottom of your Emotional Cup He will deliver you from your strongholds, your compulsions, your flesh-patterns, and even your addictions.

How does He do it?

STRATEGIES:

Changing at the
Level of Identity

CHAPTER 16

First Thing First: Grace

We are preaching a truncated version of Grace, and we are suffering terribly for it.

I trusted Christ as my savior when I was a boy of seven years old. Our pastor, Dale, would always end his sermons by inviting anyone who had never done so, to accept Christ as Savior by praying something like this: "Lord Jesus, thank you for dying for my sins on the cross; I receive you into my life the best way I know how." Simple and to the point.

I remember quite clearly that I prayed that prayer one Sunday morning. I remember quite clearly that I prayed it again the next week . . . and again the next week . . . still, again the next week, for probably six weeks in a row, until in the mind of a seven-year old I was convinced that "it took." Christ was my savior.

A few years later, when I was twelve, I went to a Christian summer camp where every morning of the week, for thirty minutes, the whole camp was to be quiet and alone as everyone read their Bibles and prayed silently. It was called the "Morning Quiet Time." One morning, when fifty or so campers and fifteen staff leaders were deadly quiet, scattered around the campground supposedly reading their Bibles and praying, I was over by the lakefront avoiding such intimacy with God. There also was another young man not seeking aloneness with God. We started talking until we began laughing out loud. (How else do you laugh?) Our laughter could be heard 'round the world. Sixty-five or so people could hear two knuckleheads down by the lake who obviously weren't reading their Bibles or praying. Good grief! We were disrupting the serenity of the whole camp.

This brought my cabin counselor suddenly out of nowhere in a swift walk toward the two of us. The other young boy was older than I, and smart enough to know that our knuckle-headedness was not welcome at this holy hour of silence, so he turned to walk away from me, in the opposite direction that the counselor cometh. He left me standing there alone, naked in my foolishness, as the counselor called out to me. He called me over to the lake's edge where we sat together on a bench.

It was the summer I turned twelve years old, 1968. Yet today, 50 years later, I still remember quite clearly what happened in those next few minutes on that bench by the lake. The counselor asked me how was my relationship with God; did He seem close to me or far away? I answered that He seemed far away. I assured him that I had already invited Christ into my heart when I was younger. I wanted to lay that fact out on the bench, so that he would know that even though I was laughing down by the lake, instead of reading my Bible, I was a born-again knucklehead.

He then asked me if I would like to alter that distance I felt with Christ and pray to invite Him to be close again. I said that I would. And so I did. I do not remember the exact words I expressed in my heart, but I remember that there was an electrical and chemical reaction in my body. God heard my prayer. He "came close." Christ was alive in me, and I knew it.

"Aha!" some of you will say, "You got saved *that* day! Those six weeks of praying as a seven-year old did not take." Yes, I know, there are some of you who would say that I did not get saved at age seven, but at age twelve, for it was then that I felt the presence of God. Others might ask about my experience at age seven, "Now, did you *really* believe? I mean, did you *really, really believe?*" I know that I was *believing* as best I could. Still, others of you will want to grill me about whether or not I truly *repented.* Did I began to *live right* after either prayer? Did I bear fruit? Did I show signs of growth? (I don't remember, but I'm sure that the next morning at camp I was reading my Bible instead of laughing down by the lake.) Ah, but did I fall away in high school? Did I become a *carnal* Christian, and if so, perhaps I was never saved until . . . *until when?* Ridiculous! To all of these well-intentioned concerns you have, I would like to say that your views reflect our truncated version of Grace.

When you believe and receive (John 1:12) the Lord Jesus Christ as your savior, your spirit is reborn from above with the life of God. Your spirit is as righteous as it will ever be. But if you do not bring your soul into the process of renewal and discipleship, as most adolescents and teenagers do not do, then your soul may not always reflect the newness that is in your spirit. But to claim that you are not a "believer-who's-going-to-heaven" because your soul still acts in corrupt fashion is to teach and practice a truncated view of Grace. Let me explain.

A major theme of this book is the difference between the spirit and the soul. A person can be born-again in the spirit, but their soul can continue to be obtuse and stubborn, and laugh down by the lake during the quiet hour. A born-again Christian can still sin, and sin quite profoundly and glaringly after being justified by grace through faith! The soul can still operate apart from God and even struggle with "slavery" to sin. In Romans 7:14 Paul said that he resembled that exactly!

The point is that your story can still have such control over your soul, that the woundedness and sinfulness of your soul can still dominate you until you do your healing work. Anyone who would judge the Apostle Paul of Romans 7:14 or another believer because of the stubbornness of their sins is judging them from the perspective of this truncated view of Grace. When we do this, we put fellow believers under the bondage of self-performing Christianity. Self-performers always end up defeated and discouraged, or if they are successful, they are enslaved to their pride. Knowing the fullness of Grace can remedy this. But let's start at the beginning.

From Genesis to Revelation justification is by grace through faith. Period. After the cross and resurrection, the content of that faith will always be something that can be reduced simply to "Jesus died for sinners, I know that I am one; I believe in His death and resurrection for me, and I receive Him as my Savior." Jesus saves, by grace through faith. We all believe that. You cannot be born-again without believing that you need to be, and that Jesus is the Author of that exchange.

He's Giving. You're Receiving. That's Grace.

But there is more to Grace than merely the unmerited favor of God. There is more to Grace than that God freely grants you at salvation that which you cannot earn or achieve. As great as that is, there is more to grace, and it can be discovered in that quiet, small letter Paul wrote to the young preacher named Titus. Paul wrote to make sure that Titus knew *how God changes and transforms the soul.* Here is what he said to Titus:

> *"For the grace of God has appeared, bringing salvation for all people, training us to renounce ungodliness and worldly passions and to live self-controlled, upright, and godly lives in the present age"* (Titus 2:11-12).

The **subject** of the sentence is Grace. The **verb** ("has appeared") is the word from which we get our word "epiphany." Paul is explaining that Grace comes to you *like an epiphany* in your heart! You find yourself believing the gospel, though you might have heard the gospel before, and even rejected it before. You find yourself believing it on the day that Grace opens the eyes of your heart to "see" the truth of the salvation message. You have an epiphany—seeing, receiving, and believing—and you are born-again.

But look. There is not a period at the end of verse 11 as some translations print. The first word in verse 12 is not capitalized (correctly in the EVS and the NASB). That first word also ends in *"ing."* That first word tells us *what* Grace began doing once it *appeared.* After it *appeared*, and granted you an epiphany, this Grace began *training you to get out of sin and to be established in righteousness.*

If you fail to see this, you will continue to be defeated by the traditional, truncated understanding of Grace. If you get this, you could get free from your frustrated inadequacy at living the Christian life.

Here's the point, again: After you have an epiphany and "see" that Grace has brought you a salvation so rich and free, then Grace begins a *second movement* in your heart. Grace begins to *train you, mentor you, guide you, and coach you* on how to turn out of sin and move toward a godly life (v 12).

Grace saves you, and then Grace trains you.

Grace saves you from your sin, and then Grace saves you from your soul!

But note this next. The word for *"instructing, training"* is the ancient Greek word used to speak of the *training of children*. It is the training and mentoring at the level of a child that is in the Apostle Paul's mind. The training is not an adult classroom speech, where Grace merely *lectures* someone to stay away from sin, and to act more righteous. No, this training is the training fit for little children. It is the kind of mentoring that tells you how, shows you how, reveals to you how, loves you if you fail now, picks you up when you fall now, opens the eyes of your heart somehow, to help you see more fully now, and always loves you through the journey, wow!

Just the way you would train a child.

Here is how the Grace of God changes you: God changes you by His powerful, invisible move upon your heart. Grace moves through reading Scripture. Grace moves as you pray. Grace moves in and through your faith, as you yield to the Spirit.

As you walk, **Grace works.**

God works a change in your life that moves you to say "No" to your former manner of living, and to begin living in the godly, righteous, sensible life of the new man. You walk, and as you start walking God works by influencing your heart, and that influence is reflected in your conduct.

So, let's review. What saves us? *Grace.* What trains us to grow in godliness? *Grace.* Grace does both.

After we are justified freely, Grace teaches us the Christian life. It trains us over the years. Grace is God in action to influence our hearts for transformed living.

Dr. Strong taught me this in his Exhaustive Concordance of the Bible. In the Greek Dictionary in the back he defines **Grace** (*charis*) as *"the divine influence upon the heart, and its reflection in the life."*

Isn't that wonderful? This is the "more" to Grace. This is the fuller definition of Grace that we are missing in most of our Bible teaching, and for that reason our lives are not changing. We need to teach Titus 2:12 more often. Here is how I like to define it:

> *Grace is God's invisible, powerful movement upon your heart, that is then manifested in your life; Grace influences and brings forth new attitudes and new behaviors.*

Back at the Cross, Grace appeared as unmerited favor, the divine bestowment of forgiveness and eternal life to undeserving sinners. That is the first grace in which we now stand (Romans 5:1), but it is not the full understanding of grace. If all we teach about Grace is the first grace, then we teach a truncated version. No wonder our lives are not being transformed! It is this second dimension that describes our journey of transformation, the work of God in renewing our soul with the life of Christ who is in our spirit. In this second dimension, Grace is still the free gift of God; still His work, and not a work of man. As we walk with God, we discover that *while* we read our Bibles and pray; *while* we listen to sermons; *while* we sing a worship song from the heart; *while* we have thoughtful dialogue with God and others; *while* we become aware of the lies in our mind and take them captive to Christ, and *while* we pray through the hurtful memories of our story and forgive others, *His invisible power is moving upon our hearts, transforming us, and His work is being reflected in our lives.* Beyond vulnerability, grace further heals us. *While* we walk, He works.

This is the grace of daily Christian living. This is the grace that I never heard growing up because we preach half of Grace. We preach that you are saved by Grace—and we do that well—but then so much of our training teaches us to become godly by being strong for God, then being stronger if you fail, or by being more committed, or by joining a small group to be accountable to help you be more committed, or by being more devoted to having devotions early in the morning like Moses did. We help you get saved by the Spirit, but then we put you to work in your own strength to achieve Christ-likeness.

We make it sound righteous by calling it "personal holiness." We read Galatians 3:3, but don't realize that we are doing the same thing that Paul scolded the Galatians for: *"Having begun by the Spirit, are you now [growing spiritually] by the works of the flesh?"*

Dear people of God, we do not produce righteousness in and of ourselves! We do not manufacture holiness on our way to being "Christ-like." We do not "create" our own

155

personal holiness. Rather, the Grace of God influences our hearts so that His holy, righteous Life is manifest *as our life.* Our holiness in daily living is His holiness, being manifested as our attitudes and conduct, by grace through faith.

One commentary that I picked up recently explained Titus 2:11-12 this way, regrettably:

*"Grace brought us salvation, and now Grace teaches us, instructs us in what is now required of us. Grace **requires** us to say no to sin and yes to right living. Grace teaches us what to do and **expects us now to do it**,"* (emphasis mine).

The editors of this book even chose a terrible subtitle: "The Requirements of Grace." Requirements? There are no requirements in grace. This is shocking! Is this an evangelical scandal? For Romans 11:6 tells us that if you add any works (*read:* requirements) to grace, **then grace is no longer grace**. This is an example of what I mean by a truncated version of Grace. This commentary rightly teaches that we are justified (declared righteous) by grace, but sadly it teaches that we grow into maturity by our own responsible achievements and works to keep the requirements of Grace. No! This is wrong! This is what keeps the Church living in defeat. You don't change yourself. This false theology is a set-up for failure.

We are not only saved by Grace, but we grow by Grace. Or we don't grow at all. Jesus said, "Apart from me you can do nothing" (John 15:5). We are either transformed by

Grace, or whatever we are doing in our own achievement counts for nothing. Grace disciples us, mentors us, meets us in dialogue about our stories, and causes us, by the power of His Life in us, to say no to sin and yes to righteousness.

He is still giving. We are still receiving. It's still Grace.

How did I forsake a nearly three-decades-long addiction? How did I quit? I can certainly tell you that I did not do it by being more committed to requirements, or by making vows to quit. In fact, I tried those. They didn't work. I kept vowing to God that I would quit . . . for 28 years! What also didn't work were the usual Christian exhortations that sounded like this:

> *You're not growing as a Christian because you are not committed enough!*
>
> *Here are 3 Things to Do . . . 5 Steps to Take . . . 6 Principles to Follow . . . that you need to do in order to please God.*
>
> *Christ gave it all, can't you strive more to obey Him this week?*
>
> *He died for you, so you better live for Him! After all He's done for you . . .*

Please quit telling people this! You are putting people under a law, a law of striving, working, failing, and frustration. The law came through Moses, but Grace and Truth came through Jesus Christ (John 1:17). Believers will quit the stronghold-enslavements that have grown out of their stories only by the wonder-working Grace of God.

In my story, I finally acknowledged the truth that I couldn't quit and mostly, I didn't want to quit. But when my wife found me out, I reeled in pain and agony, and I appeared before God with a new humility, and He changed me, for He gives grace to the humble. My humility led me to start fasting from food, to weaken my flesh so my spirit-man could rise up in power. My fasting made me hungry for God, and grace changed me. I submitted to counseling (Truth),[7] and Grace changed me. I saw my helpful Christian therapist on a weekly basis, and Grace trained me. He gave me truthful feedback on my hurtful ways of thinking, and Grace changed me. He helped me hear the truth about my self-talk and we compared it with the truth of Scripture, and Grace changed me. I finally acknowledged the truth about my interior condition: my immaturity, my anger, my poor conflict-resolution skills, and Grace changed me. Along with my therapy I prayed the truth, and Grace changed me. I read my Bible, and Grace changed me. I dialogued in the truth with God in my journal, and Grace changed me. I met with others to pray over me; we confronted the demonic, renounced generational strong-holds, healed hurtful memories, and Grace changed me. Week by week, month by month, and into the years, I

---

[7] I went to counseling for more than a few weeks! Hello? Try a few years! Most Christians fail, again, here. You go to counseling for a few weeks, a couple of months, and then quit because you don't see any change. You should try it for at least nine months to a year or longer.

confronted my lies and my self-talk, and spoke God's truth out loud. I prayed through and made changes regarding the emotional and mental truths about addiction. As I did all this, Grace changed me.

I walked, He worked. I walked in Truth through issues that I had been avoiding all my life, and Grace worked in me. The Grace of God moved upon my heart, and it was reflected in my life.

Sometimes I pulled weeds in the backyard on Saturday mornings in dialogue with God, and Grace changed me. Sometimes I would lie on my bed in agony and stare up at the ceiling wondering if my marriage would make it, and Grace changed me. *(My marriage did make it, by the way. By grace, again.)*

Grace gave me no requirements. Grace did not merely instruct me and point the way, and then shame me for failing to be more determined and devoted to personal holiness. No. In fact, Grace did not ask me to be more committed. That would be mixing grace with human achievement, and then grace would no longer be grace (Romans 11:6). Instead, as I submitted myself to the processes of healing, Grace was the leader and director of my restoration, teaching and training me in His ways.

I learned something that I had never learned before: Grace is a Person, and apart from Him I can do nothing. Prior to learning this, when striving with my addiction I was always trying to do something *for Him*. Is the church today filled with people who stopped growing long ago, because they thought they were supposed to do something *for* God? Do they live as if it were required of them to stop sinning by being more dedicated, re-dedicated, more committed, and more energized, more "fired-up," striving more, or some other such language *not found in the New Testament?* So many wonderful people have changed what they could change—to please God, or to please the pastor, or so they could qualify for some committee at the church. Today, they have hit a spiritual ceiling and stopped growing, for when their efforts could do no more, their spiritual growth stopped.

So many of us have only heard, lived, and practiced the truncated version of Grace, and we are suffering for it. We have grown accustomed to living under the bondage of our own individual strongholds, and have given up on ever changing.

Stop being more committed.

Stop re-dedicating.

Stop condemning yourself for not trying hard enough.

Start presenting yourself to God in all your glorious emptiness of the matter. Present yourself to the fullness of Grace, and allow Him to influence your heart.

This is actually the wording of Grace in the new covenant (Ezekiel 36:25-27), where God says He will give us a new heart, a new spirit, and the Holy Spirit; then He will use those three gifts to move us to obey Him. All we do is "present" ourselves to Him (Romans 12:1). This is the way we are to operate in the New Testament. committed?" Well, that sounds more like the way h... ated under the Law of Moses. The law came thro Moses, but Grace and Truth came through Jesus Chrisi. Grace and Truth. God's word reveals the truth about what needs to change, but then Grace changes it.

What are the issues of our story that need to be changed? Our Shame is most critical. Let's talk next about how God heals our Shame.

Prayer for Submitting to the Grace of the New Covenant
(Ezekiel 36:25-27)

Dear Heavenly Father,

Thank you for your Grace that both justifies me and then trains me and cleanses me from all unrighteousness. I confess that I have been a self-er, trying to be more Christ-like in my own efforts. I have been striving to live the Christian life in my own energy and effort. I repent from this. I present myself to You as a child of Grace, in submission to Your divine influence. Thank you for taking out my old heart that couldn't submit to You, and giving me a new heart to worship You, a new spirit to yield to You, and Your Spirit to transform me. Change me with Grace and Truth.

Amen.

CHAPTER 17

God's Method for Healing Shame, Part 1

"Pay attention to shame . . . because of its central role in all that ends in a curse. It is the emotional feature out of which emerges all that we call sin."

—Curt Thompson, from *The Soul of Shame*

When I was a kid I had a magic cup, one of those cups with a disappearing coin. You could buy one at any toy store. Put a nickel in the bottom, and with a sleight of hand you could look in the cup and not see the nickel. But then, magically, you could make it reappear again. Either way, the nickel was always there, but the trick was that the cup had a false bottom. Though it was called a "false" bottom, it was a very real, but separate, location in the bottom of the cup.

Let's return to our analogy of the Emotional Cup. Our Emotional Cup has a separate, deeper location at the bottom. Beneath the pain at the bottom of the cup, there is an empty space.

What you put in the bottom of the cup will determine whether or not you get well. The cup represents your *soul*; this new bottom represents your *spirit*. We have in the bottom of our cup, in our spirit, what we need for changing at the level of identity. We have God. Paul identified three unique ministries of the Trinity when he closed out the book of 2 Corinthians. In the final, farewell verse of that book he gives this benediction:

"The Grace of the Lord Jesus Christ and the love of God (the Father) and the fellowship of the Holy Spirit be with you all," (2 Corinthians 13:14).

Paul invites the Trinity to minister their unique offerings to us for our well-being. The Father has a father's love for us. He is a father to the fatherless (Psalm 68:5), and the Father from whom every family on earth is named (Ephesians 3:15). If our pain and anger came from our earthly father, then we have a Heavenly Father whose perfect love can be our comfort.

The Grace of the Lord Jesus Christ is His transforming power that works a work in us to deliver us from the broken self that our story created. His grace moves upon our hearts and brings about a change. Our transformation is by the invisible, wonder-working power of Christ (see Chapter 16).

Then, Paul does not want us to miss out on the fellowship of the Holy Spirit. It is the Holy Spirit who works out our new covenant obedience as we walk with Him.

If we quoted this verse not as a benediction but as a modern farewell expression it might read like this: *"This is the Apostle Paul signing off for now. As I close out this letter to you Corinthians, I just have this one last thing to say. Whatever you do, don't miss out on the Grace of the Lord Jesus, the love of the Father, and the companionship of the Holy Spirit."*

I remember being struck one day when this verse was pointed out to me. Here is Paul pleading with us to not miss out on a relationship with the Holy Spirit.

I was dumbstruck.

I thought to myself, "That's all I have done. My whole Sunday-School-Head-Christian life I have done exactly that: miss out on a relationship with the Holy Spirit." On that day, I believe the Holy Spirit told me how grieved He was that I had ignored His voice and His companionship. I repented and welcomed His presence in my life.

In the bottom of your cup, I encourage you to invite the three-fold ministry of the personal, covenant-keeping God of the universe.

Seek Comfort

"ALONENESS "

FEAR

ANGER

PAIN

SPIRIT'S
COMPANIONSHIP

SON'S GRACE

FATHER'S LOVE
COMPANIONSHIP

Drinking
Drugs
Pornography
Sexual Sins
Over-Eating
Lieing
Cheating
Stealing
Raging
Abusing

From the bottom of the cup, we have what we need for healing. What I learned about grace from my addiction is that God does not meet us over in the comfort-seeking behavior, to give us strength and power to overcome and stop these behaviors. No, He meets us in the bottom of the cup. He gives us power to overcome when He brings His healing love into our pain. Our story starts in the bottom of the cup. So, our healing also starts in the bottom of the cup.

God wants to meet us in our story and heal us emotionally. The bottom of the cup is where He initiates a deliverance from the sins that shame us.

I have known many people who cry out to God *in their sin*, begging for God, crying for God, to meet them *over there in their sin*, outside the cup, and deliver them from their sin. I did that. I stood in the midst of my list of comfort-seeking sins and pleaded with God to *come over there and rescue me*.

God wanted to rescue me, but His plan was different. He didn't want to meet me in my sin. He wanted to meet me in my pain, the root of the issue. He was calling me over to the place where He works, not the place where I was working to be free. The Father was waiting at the bottom of my emotional cup to begin the healing process. Finally, I joined Him there, in the place of my pain. It was the place where He started His healing work.

Comfort for the Pain

What does God want to do with my pain? He wants to comfort me. In 2 Corinthians 1:3-4, Paul used the term "comfort" five times in the two verses:

"Blessed be the God and Father of our Lord Jesus Christ, the Father of mercies and God of all comfort, Who comforts us in all our affliction, so that we may be able to comfort those who are in any affliction, with the comfort with which we ourselves are comforted by God."

Comfort. Are you kidding? What's that? We almost don't even use the word anymore. Men don't want to be comforted! Women want it, but most men don't know how to give it. It seems that only preschool children get some comfort.

But first they have to fall and skin their knee. Remember when you did that? Your mom would wash the dirt off your skin, and then blow on your skin to cool the sting. Then she would spray the antiseptic on the scrape. Again, she would blow on it because of the burning. Then a bandage was placed over the spot, and mom would hold you longer, rock you, and sing to you. This was called comfort.

We don't do comfort well, today. Lord have mercy when someone dies, and we show up at the home of the deceased with our mouths running. It's terrible—it's sad—the ridiculous things we say to the survivors gathered at the home. We very often do not comfort with our words. We are so empty when it comes to thinking of something helpful to say, because we have lost the art of giving comfort. We don't know what to do with other people's pain. Good grief, we don't know what to do with our own pain!

God knows what to do with it. He comforts it. In the bottom of your cup you have the love of the Father for comfort. But the problem—especially in my life—was that there were precious few people who know how to help me connect to the Father in such intimacy, that He might comfort me in my pain. Here's how I help people do it today.

At a Pure Heart Weekend, we give the attendees a piece of art paper and some colored markers. They are instructed to use their first-grade art skills to draw a memory on the paper. Using stick-figure-people, we instruct them to draw the scene from their memory bank of when and where they were most deeply hurt in life. The event might have been loudly traumatic. It might have been silently devastating. We want them to draw some iconic, painful memory of their moment of loneliness, rejection, abandonment, terror, or abuse. An event where, after which, they knew life might never be the same again. We pray for the Holy Spirit to bring to their hearts the memory that He is thinking of.

After everyone has drawn their picture, they return to the circle, and we begin to amplify and understand this memory better. First, I hand out a list of emotions, and have them pick out four or five associated with that memory. They write those down on the paper. Then we talk about lies, and I have them identify four or five lies they began to believe during and after that event. They write those lies down on the paper, too. Third, we have them identify the coping behaviors that grew out of that event. This could include any adult coping patterns that didn't start back then in childhood, but can definitely be traced back to the mind-set adopted from this event. They list those behaviors on the paper, too.

Our next step with this artwork is to take that memory to God in prayer. I ask the Holy Spirit to bring this memory to the counselee's mind and heart. I wait. I coach, "When you see the memory rise up in your mind, begin to describe the scene to me." So often the Holy Spirit brings forth the color, the clothing, the furniture, and other details of this hurtful memory, and we begin to discuss it. I have the counselee keep his/her eyes closed while they talk, to keep them looking with the "eyes of the heart," (Ephesians 1:18). I ask them quietly, "What do you see? Who's there? What was said? What happened? What were you feeling? What was the lie you bought? What's the truth?"

Then the Lord does His extraordinary, unusual, and mysterious work (Isaiah 28:21). The Lord invisibly, powerfully, and graciously brings comfort and healing to the person's heart.

I just did this exercise an hour ago (at the time of writing this) with a counselee. Brenda (from Chapter 4) had come to me to work on her marriage, but I could tell that she was already damaged with a shame-based identity long before she got married. I wanted to find out when her shame first emerged. This is the story she told me:

Tragically, Brenda had felt the deep pains of rejection by the boys in her neighborhood when they played Spin the Bottle. When a boy spun the bottle and it landed on her, she was immediately rejected for a kiss, with painful words of rejection. Brenda felt terribly humiliated as the boy would contort his face and declare out loud that she was too ugly to kiss. There it is. Pain! Emotional devastation! Brenda was only twelve, and sadly, it happened more than once.

In prayer, the Holy Spirit brought back to her mind the painful experience of playing Spin the Bottle in the front yard of the house next door. While we prayed she recalled the scene in her mind, feeling the pain in her heart. Then, Jesus "appeared" in the scene with her. (Since she was chosen by God before the foundations of the Earth, He was present with her at that moment in the yard.) I did not have to "suggest" that she see Jesus. I did not have to "make up" a guided manipulation of her mind. I didn't do anything except ask her what she was seeing. She said, "Jesus is there; He is hugging the little twelve-year-old me. He's telling her that He loves her; that she is worthy; that John 3:16 is true; He loves her; that she is beautiful." He told her all that. Spirit to spirit. She repeated out loud every phrase she heard Jesus say to her. I quietly wrote it all down. Brenda wept quietly in her joy.

Do you know what we call that? Comfort. This is the Comfort of God the Father. He brings to your mind a memory of when you felt alone, unloved, unwanted, fearful, rejected, or any other negative emotion. Then as you relive the memory in prayer with Him, the Lord Jesus shows up and tells you the truth of who you are. He holds you and hugs you, blows on the scrape in your heart, anoints it with His healing love, and comforts you. It's quiet. It's private. It's personal. It's life-changing.

It's the God of all comfort, comforting you, His child.

But Brenda has always been loved, right? You might argue with me, and say, "Carter, why didn't you just show it to her in the Bible, that Jesus loves her? Why do you have to do this mysterious prayer thing, you know, 'seeing' Jesus show up in the yard?" Well, I'm quite sure that Brenda had read many times already in the Bible, and been told many times in sermons, that she is loved by God. Her experience in my office did not supplant the word of God, but rather confirmed the word of God. But don't ask me why she never got comfort from the Word until in my office on this day. Perhaps on this day, because she was in prayer with all of her senses wide open, she had the eyes of her heart enlightened by the Holy Spirit to "see" that Jesus was actually with her in the yard on that day. Because He was!

All I know is that on this cool day in January, in my office, Brenda was comforted by the love of the Father, the Grace of the Lord Jesus and the companionship of the Holy Spirit. The triune God decided to meet her in her memory on this day and comfort her. Every week he uses me to facilitate the event for someone in my office or at our Pure Heart Weekends. He gives me the privilege of facilitating the gift of healing, and I help facilitate the healing of emotions. God heals. I facilitate. It's an honor and privilege to be with people, sitting in the same room with them, when they get the breakthrough of their lives, and find a Love that heals.

Glory to God. His comfort is available to you. In the next chapter I will show you how you can bring your own memories to God for His comfort.

We Put Away Anger

Now, moving up the cup, what does the Bible tell us to do with Anger? Ephesians 4:31 tells us to *"put it away."* Put your anger away. God heals the hurt with His comfort, and then you can put the anger away, when it no longer hurts.

But, first things first. You cannot put away your anger until the pain is healed, because the pain is causing the anger.

This is another area where we can be abusive, without understanding. We tell people that they need to forgive others, but we insist on it before we help them find the comfort of God for their pain. Have you ever thought about this? People can't forgive if the pain is still throbbing in their heart. Help people get comforted and healed from the pain. Then lovingly encourage them to release their anger in forgiveness.

God's Love Displaces Fear

Third, how do we get rid of Fear? How does fear leave? It gets displaced. By what? Perfect love. It says in 1 John 4:18, *"perfect love casts out (displaces) fear."* Is there any perfect love available to us? Where are we going to get some of that? Oh, yes, at the bottom of the cup. The Love of the Father is perfect. As He comforts you and heals you, then He moves into your pain and His healing presence casts out your fear. Fear evaporates in the presence of His love and acceptance.

Intimacy Replaces Aloneness

Fourth, how do we deal with Aloneness? What is the antidote to Aloneness?

Intimacy.

What emerges in your heart as you bring your hurtful memories to Christ? As He reveals where He was at those moments, as He takes your hurt upon Himself, as He comforts you and speaks to you, as you "hear his voice and follow Him" (John 10:27), what emerges? Intimacy. You and the Father, the Lord Jesus, and the Holy Spirit begin an intimate grace-walk down through the pathways of your heart. As He administers love, peace, forgiveness, and comfort to your memories, He is revealing Himself. You enter into His knowledge of you, and you "see" your true Identity in Him. He replaces the wounded identity in your soul with each healing, and brings you into a greater intimacy with Himself. This is what it means to have a personal relationship with God.

Should we really tell people that we have a personal relationship with God, when it is only an intellectual knowledge about Him and His Bible? Do you come to Him as your Shepherd? Does He make you lie down in green pastures? How does he lead you beside still waters? How does He *restore your soul* (Psalm 23)?

If you don't know how He does that, then I commend to you this chapter and the next. If you don't know the Father, Son, and Holy Spirit as your Shepherd who restores your soul, then I pray that you will boldly begin to dialogue with Him about the hurtful times in your life when you wondered where He was. Bring Him your story. Your pain. Your anger. Your fear. Your aloneness.

Instead of seeking comfort in your standard list of behaviors, turn your seeking toward Him. Invite the Love of the Father, the Grace of the Lord Jesus, and the Companionship of the Holy Spirit into your wounded journey. He will show up, because He wants to be your Shepherd. Come to the God of all comfort. In the next chapter I will show you how to do this prayer on your own.

CHAPTER 18

God's Method for Healing Shame, Part 2

A Prayer Guide for Healing Dialogue with God

Be vulnerable with friends and they will pat you on the back.
Be vulnerable with God and His love will heal your soul.
Beyond vulnerability, now get healed!

I resigned from the pastorate many years ago because of sexual sin. I hurt my wife deeply. I hurt the church. It was a very painful time.

I needed to get help, so the leaders in my life found a counseling center for pastors and their wives, where she and I could get some help. However, the center could not receive us for their intensive counseling program for another three weeks. I had to hide at home until then and hope that no one from the church came by. No one knew the details of my story, yet, and I didn't want to get cornered and have to confess to anything.

During this time the Lord led me to a book in my library that had a helpful section on healing the heart. I learned one of the greatest spiritual exercises for dealing with Shame. Let me introduce it to you in this chapter. But first, let me set the theological table.

If you are a Christian, God is present to you at all times. Further, you are a part of Him. You are a member of His body. Did you ever read 1 Corinthians 12:12 carefully? It says,

"For just as the body is one and has many members, and all the members of the body, though many, are one body, so it is with the Body of Christ."

The way most of us have heard this preached, we have made a comparison with the human body to the Body of Christ. But this verse does not mention the Body of Christ. I actually misquoted the verse above. Here is how it actually reads,

"For just as the body is one and has many members, and all the members of the body, though many, are one body, so it is with Christ."

So it is with Christ. Not, so it is with the Body of Christ, the Church. So it is with Christ, Himself. He has many members. We are members of Christ. We are not merely members of the universal body of believers called the

Church. It's more intimate than that. We are actually joined to Christ, Himself! As members of His body we are members of *Him*. We are one with Him (1 Corinthians 6:17). We are in Him, and He is in us. *"Abide in Me and I in you,"* (John 15:4).

As a believer, I am a member (a body part?) of the Second Person of the Godhead, Who is and has been present with me at all times in my life. Therefore, He is present with me *even in my memories of the past*, for He was present with me in those past events. All of my past history remains as memories in my mind, but *these are memories of events that were once present tense to me*, and God was there.

God lives outside of His creation, but is present to His creation. He created days, weeks, and years for managing life on earth (and we publish calendars to reflect this), but He is outside of time. Understand this, God lives in the eternal NOW. Everything is NOW to Him. As a result, God our Father is able to heal all the hurtful memories in my heart, no matter when they happened, for these hurtful memories from days gone by are still NOW to Him. Therefore, if He can heal them today, NOW, then I don't have to be forever bound to the wounds and rejections of my past.

As we saw with Brenda in the last chapter, the healing of these memories is essentially the spiritual work of *receiving comfort and forgiveness, granting forgiveness, breaking vows and cancelling judgments*. It is the work of healing the relationships with God, with our self, with family members and others. Such healing is provided for in the work of Christ on the cross and in the resurrection, and in His healing presence in our hearts. The cross of Christ not only applied to our sins, but to others' sins against us, and the resulting wounds as well. Have you ever noticed the words of Isaiah?

> *"Surely, He has borne our griefs, and carried our sorrows . . . He was wounded for our transgressions,"* (Isaiah 53:4-5).

Jesus carried away more than my sins and the sins of others against me. When He came to gather the sins that others did against me, He also grabbed up the pain and sorrow that their sin caused in me. He bore their sins, and He also bore my pain and sorrow. What He has borne away, I do not have to carry. I can be healed of my grief and sorrow, and this healing work is done in dialogical, healing prayer.

The *foundation* for such healing is the cross and the resurrection of Jesus Christ.

The *focus* of this healing will be receiving comfort for our hurts from the God of all comfort (2 Corinthians 1:3-6).

The *fruit of the healing* will be the dissolving of pain, anger, fear, and guilt in our hearts.

The *result* will be what the Apostle Paul calls freedom— freedom from shame and freedom to live in righteousness.

Healing prayer involves bringing the hurtful thoughts of my hurtful memories into the healing presence of Christ, and allowing Him to comfort, heal, and lift my pain away and strengthen me to stand more firmly in Christ. Consider the full understanding of these verses:

"As a mother comforts her child so I will comfort you . . ." (Isaiah 66:13).

"I will give you a new heart . . . and remove your heart of stone" (Ezekiel 36:26).

"May the Lord direct your hearts to the love of God and to the steadfastness of Christ" (2 Thessalonians 3:5)

Healing Prayer Exercise

I encourage you to confront your painful, shameful memories and receive the healing that is yours in Christ Jesus. Come out of hiding behind your story and play your God-ordained part in His bigger story. Here's an exercise that can be used to heal the hurtful memories from which the Lord wants to set you free. Begin with the following prayer:

"Dear Heavenly Father,

You desire that I have an intimacy with You for worship;

You desire that I have an intimacy with my own heart for integrity;

You desire that I have an intimacy with significant others in my life, for protection, nurture and growth.

However, the pain, anger, fear, and shame in my heart keep me from moving toward these relationships.

Please bring to my mind any event or episode in my life where I was hurt or where I hurt others; where pain came to reside instead of joy; where my emotions became frozen in unforgiveness or bitterness; or, where fear came to rule my heart.

In Jesus name, I pray.

1. As you sit quietly in prayer, ask God for a memory from your past. He knows them all, and He knows which one you are ready to deal with. Sit and listen. Wait for the Holy Spirit to bring the memory into your heart.

2. When the memory arises, still in prayer, face the hurtful memory and acknowledge the shame in your heart. "See" the event again with the eyes of your heart: Who was there? What was happening? What was said? Who hurt you? How did they hurt you? What did you do to hurt yourself or others? "See" with the eyes of your heart (Ephesians 1:18) the sin done against you, or the sin you did, in this hurtful episode.

3. Ask God what He sees in the memory, and do the appropriate spiritual work:

a. Is there a sin I have not forgiven myself for? *("See" the presence of Christ in your memory, and let Him take your sin out of your hands. Give it to Him. Receive His forgiveness.)*

b. Is there someone's sin to acknowledge and call it for what it was? *(Confess that what they did to you was sin; agree with God. Some people are fearful of disrespecting their parents by "saying" that what their parents did to them was "sinful." This would be denial if the parent's behaviors actually were abusive, shaming, or damaging mentally and emotionally. We cannot be healed if we live in denial and fantasy, and don't acknowledge the sins of others. Identify and condemn their sin, without condemning them.)*

c. Is there a deep pain and need for the Father's comfort in the memory? Is this a memory where shame flew into your heart because of your behavior or someone else's behavior against you? *("See" the presence of Christ in your memory and release to Him this shame; give Him your pain and hurt, and "see" Jesus remove it from your soul.)*

d. Is there someone to forgive? Yourself? God? *(Forgive them for the specific deeds; cancel the debt you feel they owe you; release them from needing to "pay you back" and release their sin to the cross of Christ where it should remain. Also, God doesn't need to be forgiven as humans do; He does not sin against us. However, we can certainly carry our own rift with God in our heart. In this sense I need to cancel the anger and misplaced judgment that I have against Him.*

e. Is there an image, an imagination, or a picture that is in my mind that needs to be renounced and rejected from my mind? *(Say, "I renounce that image in the name of Jesus Christ and I reject it from my mind.")* Now ask God to "re-symbolize" the location where the story happened. *(That is, ask Him to bring His glory and light into the darkness of that place, whether a bedroom, a kitchen, a classroom, under a tree at the playground, etc.)*

f. Is there a judgment I made against myself? Is there a judgment that others made that I agreed with? Do I need to renounce a bitter root of judgment against myself? *(Did you agree with someone's shame message against you? Did you curse yourself by agreeing with that judgment?)* Renounce this self-judgment by praying, "In the name of Jesus Christ, I cancel this self-judgment, and renounce this bitter root against myself, and cast it from my mind. *("See" the Lord remove the root from your heart.)*

g. Is there an attitude that I adopted on that day that needs to be renounced? *(Is this an event where I decided that I was a victim, or decided to be bitter, or adopted rebellion, or agreed with a spirit of fear; did I yield to envy, or a judgmental, critical spirit?)* Renounce this attitude in the name of Jesus.

h. In this memory is there a conviction or a lie about my identity that I agreed with and need to renounce and reject—perhaps a lie someone or Satan told me about myself on that day? *(Cancel the specific lie in the name of Jesus; arrest it and take it prisoner; turn it over to Christ. Did this event convince me of the lie that I am worthless, unwanted, unloved, unacceptable, a born-loser, a reject, a bad person, etc.?)* Renounce and reject that lie from your mind and heart in the name of Jesus Christ.

i. Finally, is there a truth from God that can replace that lie? (Listen to the Holy Spirit speak to you; let Him speak the Father's love to you. Listen. What do you hear? What do you think you hear? He will speak into your heart.)

4. Record this prayer-time in a journal. Then continue to "speak what you believe" (2 Corinthians 4:13). Daily confess this new truth spoken to you by the Holy Spirit. Do not continue to give Shame a foothold.

REMEMBER: *Forgiveness* is not forgetting about the event. There are certain, painful events that we will never forget. Instead, forgiveness is a choice to receive a miracle work of God in your heart. In this miracle you agree to cancel the debt you feel that another owes you, and live with the consequences of his/her actions. As a result of this miracle, bitterness is released. You acknowledge your hurt and your hate, but you first accept the healing comfort of God, and then you let the other person go. Please note well: *forgiveness is always preceded by God first healing the hurt in your heart. Intimacy precedes activity. Intimacy with God in regard to your pain precedes your work of forgiveness.*

5. Close with this final prayer:

> Dear Heavenly Father,
>
> I thank You for the Healing Power that is in the Cross and Resurrection. Thank You for the gift of dialogue and Your invitation to tell You where I am. I have unnecessarily carried this pain for too long. I pray that You will redeem the time lost and empower me for new steps in walking out this freedom, expressing new worship to You, new integrity with myself, and new intimacy with others. Lord Jesus, thank You for your transforming grace; and Holy Spirit, continue to express Christ's life through me.
>
> In His Name.

During those dark days of my life after I resigned from the ministry, I got on my knees every day for several weeks and asked Father to grant that the Holy Spirit would reveal a memory from my past, one memory every day. In my case, God worked chronologically backwards from the present day to my early childhood, but He may do it differently for you. Every day in prayer He brought forth a memory, and as it emerged in my heart I saw it in my mind's eyes. I remembered some of them in clear detail, in living color. As I "saw" them in my heart, I would process each one as I outlined above. I forgave myself if it was a sin I did to another person. I forgave others if they had hurt me. I renounced bitter self-judgments, and renounced attitudes I had adopted. I rejected lies that I "bought" on the day of that memorable event. I commanded demonic spirits to depart from my presence. I listened to the Holy Spirit speak a new identity over me.

Day by day I dealt with the history of my heart's journey, walking back through the places where in my own mind I formed and fashioned a shame-based identity. Day after day I replaced those thoughts with new ones from Father. My true self slowly emerged in the grace-based identity of the Holy Spirit's words over me.

Stan came on one of our Pure Heart Weekends. On this retreat we train people in the prayer exercise above, and mentor healing and freedom to those struggling with strongholds. On the final day of the retreat, I explained the Memory-A-Day prayer exercise, and encouraged the participants to continue healing their own hearts after they go home from the retreat.

Stan had a powerful retreat experience, and he came home exuberant about what God had done in his heart. After a few weeks, however, he was off his emotional high, and he was struggling mightily again with his flesh. Then he recalled the Memory-A-Day prayer exercise, and, well . . . here's what he said to me:

> *Carter,*
>
> *I have to admit to you, that when you shared your experience of the Memory-A-Day exercise, it sounded like something I would never do. It sounded like something a preacher-boy would do, but not what a former football player would do.*
>
> *But you know, I got desperate. I grieved that I had lost the joy and power that I came home with from the retreat. So, I got out my journal, read through the exercise, and I started doing it!*
>
> *I did it daily for a few weeks, and it changed my life!*
>
> *Thank you so much for teaching it at the retreat.*

It works. I hope you will do it, too. In James 4:8, God tells us to purify our hearts. Most of us think that refers only to sins. But our hearts are full of lies, attitudes, hurt words that others have said to us, harsh words that our parents once yelled at us, rejection from people we hoped would accept us, and more. There is so much more that needs to be purified from our hearts than just sinful behaviors. This prayer exercise can help. It can cause the shameful-self to fall away, and our new identity *in Christ* to emerge stronger in our spirit.

There is a secondary tool to deal with Shame, and it should follow subsequently to dealing with it in prayer. After you and God walk through your story for His healing, then you should share your story with a few trusted, safe people. We heal when we get our secrets out. We heal further when we tell our story. There are four benefits to telling your story.

1. *The more you tell your story, the more you understand it.* Understanding the story of your life is powerful to help you get healed. When you can identify the tragic moments of your life, then you can see where your identity was malformed in your soul. The more you understand your story the more you can identify the toxic emotions, the lies and the attitudes you adopted. You then understand not just *what* you have done in response to it all, but you understand *why* you have done what you've done. Journal your story. Re-read it. Own it. Know the journey of your heart.

2. *The more you tell your story, the more healing you get from it.* Every time you tell your story, it hurts a little less. Remember the time someone told you a funny joke, and you laughed and laughed yourself silly! Then you told the joke later to a friend, and you both laughed and laughed. The second time you told it you laughed. The third time you told it you grinned and giggled. The fourth time you told it you merely grinned. The fifth time you told it you just smiled and enjoyed the others who were now laughing themselves silly! With each telling of the joke, the power of the humor wore off, and it had less and less of an influence on your own laughter. In a similar (but opposite) way, the first time you tell your story it might be painful and scary, and you might choke up with emotion. However, with each telling of your story, the power of the pain wears

off, the fear wears off, and it has less and less of a shaming influence over you. You are healed more with each telling.

3. *The more you tell your story, the more freedom you get from the shame.* Every time you tell your story, you get a little freer. You get more freedom from the shame, from the pain, from the humiliation, from the frustration, from the powerlessness, etc. With each telling of the story, you get more freedom from the negative, painful emotions that the memories have had over you.

4. *Finally, the more you tell your story, the more power you get over it.* Every time you tell your story to a safe person, the more you begin to reign over it. As you understand it more, heal from it more, and gain more freedom from it, then the more power you get over it. You begin to own this story. It doesn't own you so much. The conversations in your head are changing, and you are walking in the Spirit of Life in Christ Jesus over the story of sin and death.

Over the next years, tell your story and tell your story; then tell your story some more. Tell it to a friend over coffee. Then tell another friend, too. Tell your story at an appropriate place in the Bible study group. Tell it on the retreat to your break-out group. Tell it to your roommate late at night on that retreat. Tell it to a family member on a private walk at the family reunion.

Tell it appropriately. Tell it respectfully. Tell it honestly and authentically. Don't tell it as a victim. Tell it as someone who has been healed, is still being healed, and is growing in the grace of Christ's healing presence in your life.

Some people are confused about their own painful story, but hearing you tell your story could give them clarity for their faith. Some people are hurting, and telling your story will bring them hope, while at the same time continue to heal you more. Some people can't feel the love of God, but they can draw near as they hear you tell your story of how God showed up in your memory and lovingly healed you.

Tell it cautiously, because some people are dangerous and not trustworthy. Don't tell it to those people. Some crowds are not the right place. Be careful. Your story is valuable, and it's not for everyone. It's a pearl so don't share it with the swine.

Shame begins to dispel when we share our story with safe people who love us. Shame grows in our secrets. We are healed from the shame when we tell our secrets to safe people.

Addicts have group meetings. Then they go out for coffee afterwards. You know what they do at the meetings and at coffee? They share their stories, and they understand their lives better. They get healed. They get free. They grow in power over their stories. The old story loses its grip over them, as they own it and live out a new story.

My story used to lead me to disobedience and disappointment with Christ. Now, after many years of telling my story, I understand it. I continue to be healed. I continue to get free from it, as I continue to have power over it. With Christ as my life, I own the story! It no longer owns me.

Come out of your hiding. Let others in on the story, and Christ will heal you further, beyond your dialogical, listening prayers with Him. Now that your story is losing its grip on you, let's talk about how to reign over that story.

CHAPTER 19

Reign over Your Past

Whoever will reign with Christ on earth must drive passivity from the seat of authority.

After resigning from the ministry, I, of course, went into counseling. One session, several months into the process, the counselor tore off a large sheet of paper from an easel pad and laid it on the floor. He handed me a felt-tip marker.

"I want you to write down a list of everything that you are passive with in your life," he said. "Make a list of all the issues, conflicts, and relationships about which you are passive."

He had me get down on the floor like a little kid, and hover over the large sheet of paper as I wrote. The room was quiet. I took the marker in my hand and I began to think. *What have I been passive about? Where do I take a back seat to others? Where do I let others take control?* Then I began to write a list.

◆ I remember when I went to Europe with a bunch of guys after college. One night in Paris we were taking the subway trains around the city; the other guys were so intent on proving who was better at reading French, who was better at reading the directions in the subway, running ahead to look at the map and determining which trains, which routes and which streets to take; that I merely stood back and followed them, never caring one whit about looking at the map. I fully trusted in their competitiveness to lead us in the right direction. I was completely passive, and had a wonderful time!

Wait a minute . . . I think I might be missing the point of the exercise. Passivity is supposed to be a negative thing . . . let's see . . .

◆ Oh, yeah, in my marriage I was passive to my wife's assertiveness, which I self-righteously decided was actually aggressiveness; thus, I was right to be passive and let her be the bigger sinner (!).

◆ I was passive in college and seminary days, letting others have their way, even making a destructive theology in my mind: *I need to let others have their way, because if they get mad about life, they will "quit on God." However, I will never quit on God, so I'll let them have their way to help them out spiritually.*

Hmmmm . . . that might be unhealthy, you think?

- With my children, I was passive about disciplining and training them; I let my wife do most of it. If I got irritated with them I would stuff, stuff, stuff some more, then blow up at them!

- I was passive in the face of conflict, which meant that I would let others take advantage of me.

Ah-ha! I was beginning to catch-on to the point of this exercise, now. No wonder I had a lot of suppressed anger in my life. I let others have their way, and had no respect for myself. I taught others that they could take advantage of me! Wow, that stings. I did not love myself enough to stand up for myself. My passivity was producing internal rage! Whoa, now.

But wait, I saw even more.

- I was passive in the schoolyard as an adolescent; never standing up to any bully.

- I was passive in relationships; if I liked a girl and she didn't like me, I didn't try to talk to her or win her over; I just let it go and walked away, alone again.

- I let others on the basketball team intimidate me, and lost my starting role.

- Let's see . . . I was passive about . . . . I was passive . . . . I was . . .

Then it hit me. I dropped the magic marker, and rolled over on my back. I stared at the ceiling, speechless. Stunned. My eyes were wide-open: *I was passive with the addiction in my life.* I had let the addiction roll over me and take control of me. I didn't fight it. I didn't fight for freedom. I didn't fight to be under the control of the Holy Spirit. And why not? Because over the years of passivity, as I *taught* others to disrespect me, I had come to disrespect myself. I subconsciously believed I was unworthy of being free of the addiction, unworthy of a starting role on the team, unworthy of any girl's attention, unworthy of standing my ground, unworthy of being assertive, unworthy of walking in the power of my identity in Christ!

I was living as a victim in regard to much of my life! I claimed to be a victim; that strong powers outside my control had made me who I was; that other people were bullies; that mean people had given me no choice; that I was a victim to their immaturity and selfishness; that other people were in the way of my success; that God had made me inferior to others; poor pitiful me!

But I was not a victim. It was my fault!

It was my fault that others won and that I lost. It was my fault that I was trapped in my stronghold addiction. My story was the story of my passive victimhood!

Now, note that **being** a victim and **living as** a victim are two different things. *Being a victim* is usually not a choice, as it is something that can happen to anyone when, say, you are rear-ended at a red light, your house is broken into, your father has an affair leading to your parents' divorce. Bad things can happen to anyone, making that person a momentary victim. But *living as a victim* is a choice. It is an intentional identity; it implies a lifestyle; that a mindset has been adopted. Victimhood is a prison that we choose. When the offense becomes your identity, you are now *living as a victim.*

You have received it.

You believe it.

And now you speak it.

You're in a prison.

A victim is defeated, and I was living as one. I had grown to be a coward and had quit fighting for my heart. I would not fight for spiritual renewal, nor read the Scriptures with an open heart to be changed. I would not fight to cancel out my defeating conversations that played in my head. I would not fight to forgive others, fight to live in self-awareness, fight to submit to God. I would not tell the demonic to shut up and leave. I claimed to be helpless. I claimed I had no other options. I showed up to church where I preached and counseled with God's Word, but I was passive.

I never saw my passivity! Therefore, I never did anything about it.

You cannot live as a passive victim and hope to overcome the shame of your back-stories. After you do the healing of your emotional cup, and as you are healing a memory-a-day, you must not continue to live as a victim. Out of your healing, you must come out of your passivity toward your destructive flesh patterns.

Passivity is the Fuel of our Flesh

As we already have pointed out, it's not just addicts who struggle with strongholds. From the pastor down to the volunteer nursery worker, everyone has some sinful, selfish behavior, some controlling thought or attitude which they are deeply committed to. Everyone is doing something to protect, provide for, self-promote, or pleasure oneself. Your backstory has driven it, but you continue to do it despite praying for God to help you quit—or not even "seeing" it to pray about it!

What are you passive about?

What behavior or attitude have you been confronted with but done nothing about?

Surely, you have been confronted by God, by your spouse, by your children, by a sermon, or even by a friend's testimony, about destructive habits or ways of operating in your own life. You've seen that something needs to change, but you've done nothing about it. To this degree is your Christian life simply fraudulent!

When we live as a victim, we are telling ourselves that our stronghold patterns of selfish behavior are permitted because of what happened to us in the past. We can't help it.

But we are not reigning in life!

If we are ever to get well spiritually and stop our destructive behaviors, we will have to confront our victim-mentality and passivity, call it for what it is, and declare holy war on it.[8] We must reject victimhood and passivity. We must choose to live and reign in our new identity in Christ.

The opposite of victimhood and passivity is reigning with Christ as my life. Have you ever noticed the final line of Romans 5:17? *"But those who receive the abundance of grace and the free gift of righteousness will reign in life through Christ Jesus . . ."*

"Reign in life." Now there's a novel concept for the Victim. I had read that verse a hundred times and never saw the power of that last phrase, *"reign in life."* One translation reads, *"reign as kings in life."* Instead of letting our circumstances reign over us, instead of letting the past reign over us, instead of letting our thoughts and our emotions reign over us in passivity, *we can reign over them!*

How do we reign in life?

How do we take the grace and righteousness of Christ and reign in life?

Reigning in life requires authority, the authority of a king.

Our Identity in Christ Includes His Authority

God used three different functional individuals in the Old Testament to lead the people of Israel. These three leaders were the Prophet, the Priest, and the King. When

---

[8] Remember, our battle is not against flesh and blood (Ephesians 6), nor with the weapons of flesh, but is fought with the spiritually powerful weapons of God (2 Corinthians 10:3-4).

Christ came to earth it has been noted that He functioned in all three of these offices, too. But He was greater! Christ did not just bring the Word of God as a prophet, He *was* the Word of God. Christ did not merely intercede for people to the Father like a priest, He was both the offering for sin, and the high priest who offered it. Third, Christ was not merely a king to deliver His people from the enemy, but He triumphed over the enemy permanently, and is now the King of Kings.

In the church today, as His Body, we also minister in these three offices. With the gifts of teaching and preaching the Bible, we carry on a **prophetic** ministry to one another. When we minister to one another in prayer, praise, and worship we have a **priestly** ministry to one another.

But is there a way that we function today as kings? How do we carry out a kingly role in the church today as a community of believers? To answer that, let's look at what the kings did in ancient Israel.

In the Old Testament the king was not required to legislate new laws. God had already laid down His Law, and the priests and judges merely administered the Law of Moses. Therefore, the major function of a king was authority in the command of an army to battle the enemy, to take back any ground that the enemy had usurped, and to tear down the altars and idols of spiritual enemies. In the case of one king in particular, King David, the authority of the kingly office was manifested early in his life in three ways:

- He was **aware of his authority** when only an adolescent;

- He **spoke and commanded with the certainty** of that authority;

- and He operated in his authority with a bold **fearlessness**.

We see this in 1 Samuel 17, when we read the story of David and Goliath. It began with David arriving at the front lines bringing food for his brothers who were soldiers in the army of Israel. The nation was engaged in a battle with the Philistines, and both armies were lined up on opposite sides of the valley. The battleground stood empty between them, for something strange was going on. There was no fighting. Both armies were standing idle, and they had been like this for forty days!

Every morning the giant, Goliath, would step down into the floor of the valley to taunt the Israeli army, and to challenge them to a one-on-one battle with him, winner takes all.

The scene was dismal. The soldiers of Israel slunk away in dismay and great fear (v. 11) at the sight of this intimidating figure. The Israelite army as a whole was living in fear and passivity. They were victims to a bully in the valley.

Then David showed up.

When he saw and heard the giant for the first time, look at his reaction (v. 26). In contrast to the whole Israelite army, David seethed in anger. *"Who is this uncircumcised Philistine, that he should defy the armies of the living God?"*

His attitude was like, "He can't talk like that about God!" David got an audience with King Saul, and told him he could kill that giant. For he had killed a lion and a bear with his own simple weapons, and he would be glad to strike down this "uncircumcised Philistine" for wagging his tongue against the armies of the living God. Eventually Saul granted permission, and David gathered his sling and five stones, and walked out onto the floor of the valley, in view of the giant.

When Goliath saw him he mocked David and cursed him by the gods of Philistia (v. 43), but David yelled back at him with authority.

"You come to me with a sword, a spear, and a javelin, but I come to you in the name of the Lord of hosts, the God of the armies of Israel, whom you have defied.

This day the Lord will deliver you into my hand, and I will strike you down and cut off your head. . . . that all the earth may know that there is a God in Israel, and that all this assembly may know that the Lord saves not with the sword and spear.

For the battle is the Lord's and He will give you into our hand," (1 Samuel 17:46,47).

When the giant moved toward the young teen, David ran! He ran straight toward the giant to meet him at the battle line. He acted as a king with the authority of God, and he struck down the giant and cut off his head, just as he said he would do!

This is a king, doing a king's business. From this we see the same three points.

1. Kings act in the power of their God-given authority: *"I come to you in the name of the Lord of Hosts . . . for the battle is the Lord's, and He will give you into our hand,"* (v 47).

2. Kings do not beg or ask for permission, they command and decree: *"This day the Lord will deliver you into my hand, and I will strike you down and cut off your head,"* (v.46).

3. Kings are bold and fearless in their authority: *"David ran quickly toward the battle line to meet Goliath,"* (v 48).

David was the youngest man in the valley that day, but he didn't tremble with fear as his brothers did. He didn't operate his life in passivity. He came upon the battlefield and observed the taunts of the giant, and his immediate response was outrage! Righteous anger! *"You can't put this reproach on the nation of Israel! You can't defy the armies of the living God! You can't say that!"*

For forty days the two armies stood opposite one another in a staring contest, but the whole ordeal was over and done in five minutes when someone who walked in authority showed up in the valley. This is the office of the king, and it is what we need in our churches today. We need believers who have advanced in their spiritual maturity through the exercise of their kingly authority. We need more spiritually mature people who can restore people caught up in sin (Galatians 6:1), and who can snatch people from the fire (Jude 23)! We need more who have found their authority in Christ over their own story, over their own passivity and fear; who have defeated their own enemies, cut off their heads, and who walk in power and authority.

Do you reign in life with Jesus Christ, or does your story still reign over you? Do you reign with this kind of authority, or do you remain passive about your strongholds?

Our victory comes in learning to walk in power and authority over our enemies, and the story our enemies are trying to tell about our lives. Let's talk about how to do that, next.

CHAPTER 20

Reign over Your Mind, Emotions, and the Demonic

Joshua told the field commanders, "Come here. Put your feet on the necks of these kings." They stepped up and put their feet on their necks. Joshua told them, "Don't hold back. Don't be timid. Be strong! Be confident! This is what God will do to all your enemies when you fight them."

—Joshua 10:24-25, MSG

In my own journey out of addiction and into freedom, I had to learn to take authority over anything that was hindering the healing and freedom process. By receiving the grace of God and the gift of righteousness (Romans 5:17a) we as believers have new credentials. We have the power and authority of Christ to reign in life as co-regents with Him: *But he who receives the abundance of grace, and the gift of righteousness shall reign in life through Jesus Christ,"* (Romans 5:17b).

What do we reign over in this life? We reign over our past.

We reign over our thoughts and the conversations that play in our heads. We don't have to let our emotions rule over us. We can change our stubborn flesh patterns, and take authority over the demonic.

We reign over our shame, so our stories no longer have more control over us than God does. We reign over our stories and everything from which Christ came to set us free!

Let's talk about how to take authority over our mind, emotions, and our behavior, as well as over the demonic, and let me use three other people to illustrate each of these areas.

Dealing with Old Childhood Messages of Shame

I was just interrupted while writing this chapter by a phone call from a friend in Texas. Craig is a police officer. He, too, was another man who grew up as a boy receiving messages from his parents and struggling with memories that made him feel inadequate, never good enough, and never affirmed. We have counseled by phone for a couple of years now, getting out of his shame-based identity ("Pending Approval"), and into his identity in Christ ("Approved and Accepted in the Lord").

Today, on the phone, he told me of the stress in his life over three things: his meager paycheck, his wife's smaller income, and the emotional difficulty of his young son. Then, to top it off—a gunman had taken a shot at him the other night on patrol, and he realized, "Wait a minute . . . My salary is not big enough to expose myself to flying bullets!"

As we talked, it became clear that the major issue was the monologue in his head. Craig hears the old conversations of his shame-based identity: *"You're not good enough; you blew it years ago when you should have joined the Navy; you're not smart enough to do anything to make more money; you are not providing well for your family; you're a failure."*

Previously, Craig and I had done a few prayer sessions for healing some old hurtful memories. Second, we had looked at his new identity as found in Ephesians 1. Today, he needs to stand firm in this new identity work that Christ has already begun in him. He needs to stand firm in what the Lord did in his heart and mind in our recent memory-prayer work. Most importantly, he needs to renounce every message from the monologue of shame that arises in his mind, and let the Holy Spirit speak his true identity into his heart.

Renounce it. Reject it. Speak the truth.

We take control over the thoughts of our mind when we realize "whose voice" is speaking these negative thoughts. Is that my father? Is that my failure? Is that my shame? Confront that voice and speak what is true. Contradict that voice with Scripture. Speak your identity from our list in Chapter 11. Speak it out loud. We can diminish the power of our negative emotions when we speak our true identity in Christ.

I said to Craig, "Take authority over those thoughts. Don't let them own you. Don't let them have you. Have them, instead! Arrest them. Take them captive to Christ, so He can dismiss them."

"We destroy arguments and every lofty opinion raised against the knowledge of God, and take every thought captive to obey Christ. . . ." (2 Corinthians 10:5).

Notice the last phrase, "take every thought." You can't take any thought to Christ that you don't recognize to take. You must do your backstory work to discover the lies of your shame. Then take authority over them. Command those lies to fall to the ground. Let Christ, Who is the Truth, speak His very words from Ephesians 1 over you. Take authority with Truth, and speak who Christ declares you to be.

Dealing with Undesirable Images

Sandy came to me because her husband had committed adultery with another woman that Sandy knew well. The interaction between her husband and this woman began with the exchange of sexual images on the phone. Sandy did not see the images, but she forced her husband to confess what words were texted and what body images were photographed. Once they were in counseling, her husband also confessed to how many times and where (locations) the affair was carried out. It is necessary for the offender's healing to tell all the truth. His secrets must come out. This also allows the offended spouse to get all of her nagging questions answered, so she too can start her healing process.

However, this always leads to the unfortunate state of mind where Sandy found herself when she came to me. For now she had "vain imaginations" stamped upon her brain. For as her husband described the texts and the trysts, Sandy made up "images" in her mind as she listened. She pictured all of it in her mind, and made up "movie trailers" as she heard the details. Sandy made up images of the other woman's body, the woman's face as she took and received pictures of Sandy's husband, and as she lay with Sandy's husband. She made up in her mind images of her husband's face as he saw the "sexting" photos; his face as he took selfies, and his face as he lay with the other woman. She created imaginary photos in her mind of their secret rendezvous.

She couldn't help it! She couldn't help but see it. Our brains work that way due to our curious imagination, and it can lead to haunting images that torture the healing and recovery from the affair of a spouse. I led Sandy in a prayer like this:

"Dear Lord Jesus,

Though I had to know the truth, and my husband had to tell the truth to start our healing process, I hate these images that are in my mind.

I ask you, Holy Spirit, to bring up before my mind's eyes every vain image that I have created in my mind, that I might renounce and reject it from having power over me."

As Sandy waited, the Holy Spirit then began to bring up each "vain imagination" to the eyes of her heart. With every image that arose, I coached Sandy to say, "I renounce that image in Jesus' name, and I reject it from my mind."

She did this several times over the next few minutes, until no more images arose. Sandy took authority over those images. She renewed her mind, and then asked the blood of the Lord Jesus to wash over her brain, cleanse it from the unrighteousness of these images, and then asked the Holy Spirit to repossess those places on her brain and in her mind, and seal them off as holy ground. Sandy commanded boldly, took authority, and reclaimed the "land" that the enemy had usurped.

What horrible images and memories do you carry in your mind? Childhood memories of abuse or some trauma? Pornography images that torture you? Memories of things you regret? Take authority over them. Renounce them each, one by one, and reject them from your mind. Use Sandy's prayer and take authority over your mind.

Dealing with Demonic Strongholds

Sam came to see me for counseling because he was struggling to love his wife. His heart seemed empty, even cold. He couldn't express warmth and compassion toward her, but he didn't know why. He sat down across from my desk and I opened with a strong prayer, a prayer with the vocabulary of spiritual warfare and authority. When my prayer was over, I asked Sam if he felt anything in his heart, or sensed anything in his body while I was praying.

Surprised at my question, he responded with a yes. He said, "While you were praying I felt like two cold hands came up and covered my heart, as if to hide and shield my heart from you."

I inquired, "How long have you felt like these two hands have controlled your heart with coldness? When do you think it happened?"

He knew exactly when. "My father died when I was only eleven years old. I was the youngest of four brothers, and at the wake, the night before the funeral, my brothers and I were sitting in a row in the funeral home chapel, and I was sobbing in tears. My uncle came walking by and looked down at me, and said something like this, '*Boy, quit your crying right now. Stop crying and be strong. Be a man.*' So, I did. I quit crying. I stuffed my sorrow and grieving, and shut down my heart from feeling any more pain."

From that day, Sam had been a man who couldn't connect emotionally and warmly, and now he was emotionally detached from his wife. He was a stoic man, limited in his emotional capacity.

I said, "Put your hands over your heart and repeat after me," and I led Sam in the following words:

In the name of Jesus Christ, as a holy, righteous child of God, I am covered by the blood of the Lord Jesus and filled with His resurrection life.

By His power and His authority, which I share in, I command you, demonic spirit, to loose yourself from me.

Leave me now and go to Jesus Christ for your judgment.

We paused, and then I asked, "Is it still there?" He sat still for a moment and then nodded, "Yes." I said, "Let's command again," and we repeated the declaration and command. We paused again, and I asked a second time if it were still there. He said, "Yes, it's still there." So, now, I got a little more forceful. No more "repeat after me." From across the desk I spoke with a stronger authority from my faith. I commanded that demon to loose itself from Sam right now, and leave in the name of Jesus Christ!

Suddenly, Sam's face changed to the color of peace. He said, "It's gone. It's gone . . . oh, wow! . . . peace is slowly pouring down through me . . . inside me . . . like oil. Oh, wow. Oh, wow! The peace of Christ is filling my head . . . like everything I have to do today is being pushed back . . . nothing is important but this peace . . . now it's pouring down slowly into my heart . . . anxiousness is leaving . . . I am at peace. There is nothing important in my heart but the Lord . . . and to love my wife. It's gone . . . I'm free."

How did that demonic spirit come to leave?[9] What made it leave? First, Sam and I recognized its presence. Then we took authority over it, an authority that is from Christ, and is available to work through us because we are one with Him. The authority is, of course, Christ Himself. I had met a few demons in my counseling before, and I knew that I could speak with the authority of Christ to send the demon packing. When I got firmer (angrier?) and spoke with more conviction out of my authority, the demon knew that I meant business. I had authority over him, but when that demon realized that *I knew I had authority over him*, it left!

Sam and I *reigned in life* that day (Romans 5:17). We reigned with the kingly authority of Christ, the King, who is our life. We spent the rest of our counseling session learning how to reign over his "dead" emotions, and talked about how to move toward his wife with affection and connection.

---

[9] In the Gospels, the word used most often to refer to people who were harassed or under the influence of demons is a word that is best translated, "demonized." There is plenty of good material on this subject, and I don't have anything new to add to it. I will just emphasize its importance. On the journey of battling strongholds, one must always take one day in your life to meet with someone who knows their authority over the demonic, and let this person minister freedom and deliverance for you, as well as teach you how to walk on your own in the authority of Christ.

A Strategy for Taking Authority over Your Mind and Emotions

Our story of shame can get triggered easily by other people's offenses against us, and by intrusive thoughts from our unrenewed mind. When your emotions rise up in fear, anger, guilt, shame, pride, arrogance, or pouting, then you must first realize that these emotions are not lying to you. Emotions never lie, only my thoughts can be lies. I know! We've been told for generations that our emotions can't be trusted; however, now we are learning the real truth: *Our emotions are the truest, most certain thing going on inside of us at any moment. Our thoughts are the real problem, because our thoughts essentially "create" our emotional state. Thus, instead of lying, our emotions actually "tell us" what we are thinking. Once we discover what we are thinking, then we can take our thoughts captive to Christ for the renewing of our mind.*

We all know that confusion, denial, and rationalization originate in our minds. Thus, the mind—at any given moment—could be the most confusing place on planet Earth! It sometimes is difficult to get our hands around what we are thinking during emotionally powerful moments, particularly in moments of pain and anger. Thus, a key to the renewing of your mind should sometimes begin with the feeling of your emotions. Let the Holy Spirit guide you from that emotion, up to your mind to discover the thought behind the emotion. Then the Holy Spirit and the Scripture can expose whether your thought is flowing from the mind of Christ or from the mind set on the flesh (your shame-based identity). This requires listening and humbly receiving whatever it is that the Spirit has to say to you.

Isn't this what King David was praying for when he asked God to reveal "any hurtful way in me" (Psalm 139:24)? Hurtful ways start with hurtful thoughts. Once you discover that what you're thinking, for instance, is *erroneous, self-condemning, critical or arrogant,* it is your responsibility to take authority over those thoughts. When you do not give them space in your mind, then you can better control your emotions.

As we just said, our emotions come from our thoughts; thus, toxic emotions come from our toxic thinking. By His grace, if you are controlling your mind and your emotions, then you will have more power for controlling your behaviors. This practice of taking authority over your emotions and thoughts is called the *renewing of the mind* (Romans 12:2). When we add to it a change in behavior, it is called walking in the Spirit (Galatians 5:25-6:1).

Here's a strategy for taking authority over your mind, your toxic emotions, and ultimately your hurtful behaviors.

1. Feel your feelings, and feel them well. That is, on the way to the refrigerator to eat more; on the way to the top shelf to drink more; on the way to the computer to turn on porn; on the way to confront someone and give them a piece of your mind; on the way to writing an email to "nail" someone for their mistaken notions; on the way to the front of the church to tell "your side of the story" to the pastor;

on the way to the meeting to deliver a speech you have rehearsed over and over to justify yourself and prove others wrong; on the way to your in-laws' house to tell them to butt out of your business— Stop! Stop and feel your feelings, and feel them well.

2. Identify your feelings, but then feel a little deeper. Remember this: anger is a secondary emotion. If you are feeling anger, then it arrived second. Some other emotion came first, so feel below the anger to discover your primary emotion. It will be some form of pain (see The Emotional Cup). Below your anger is some painful, hurtful emotion such as: *sadness, shame, disappointment, embarrassment, humiliation, loneliness, regret, misunderstanding, pressure, unloved, unappreciated, un-affirmed, emasculated, used, violated or disrespected,* to name a few. Get below your anger to feel the painful feelings, and discover the painful emotion that is driving you.

3. Telegram! That painful emotion has a telegram for you telling you what is going on inside of your head; what it is that you are thinking. Every emotion has a message, a "telegram" attached to it. That telegram corresponds to the thought in your mind that is "creating" the emotion. Feel your feeling until you discern its message.

4. Now, arrest that message. Take hold of that thought/belief/opinion and take it captive to obey Christ (2 Corinthians 10:5), i.e., bring that thought

into the kingdom of God as His subject. Bring that message into the light of God and His Word.

5. Then listen as the Spirit searches and speaks to you. Is this message true? Is this message false? Is it an accusation against you? Is it a charge against you? Is it a condemnation of you? Whose voice are you hearing? Is it the old conversation of your Shame-Based Identity? Is it an attack on your true identity in Christ? Does this message cause you to doubt God's goodness or His love and acceptance of you?

6. Then take authority over this message and tear it down with the weapons of God (His grace; His truth; His love; His acceptance). Renew your mind with Scripture, which will renew your emotions, which will grant you more control over your behaviors. Now, you are walking in authority and triumph in Christ.

Remember, as we pointed out in Chapter 12, one of the greatest weapons of God is *Spirit-taught truth*. When the Holy Spirit reveals scriptural truth to your heart and opens the eyes of your heart to "see" it (Ephesians 1:18), then you are experiencing one of the mysterious blessings of the New Covenant: God is writing His word on your heart.

In Jeremiah 31:33 Yahweh says about our new covenant relationship with Him, *"I will put my law within them, and I will write it on their hearts."* When the Holy Spirit opens the eyes of your heart to see the hope of your calling (Ephesians 1:18), the Holy Spirit is writing on your heart. He is teaching you what you've been reading in Scripture.

Receive it.

Believe it.

Speak it.

Add to this the reference in Ephesians 6:17, where we are instructed to take up *"the sword of the Spirit, which is the Word of God."* This phrasing in the Greek language is telling us that the sword, which is given by the Spirit, is the *rhema* word of God. A *rhema* word is when the Holy Spirit speaks a personal word from Scripture for your situation. Thus, the sword of the Spirit is Spirit-taught truth. The sword for reigning over your backstory is the power and conviction of the truth of God's word, which you possess firmly from the Holy Spirit, revealing and confirming it to you in your situation. Remember, when the Holy Spirit teaches you something, you've got it. You don't have to take notes!

There is another thing we can do with our mouth to walk in power and authority over our story. Let's talk about that next.

CHAPTER 21

Confess Your Way to A New Future

Our authority is voice-activated; use your mouth to change your life!

Y our story does not have to reign over you. You were not created to live a defeated life, where your story has more control over your life than God does.

Your original design was to be a co-regent over creation with God, evidenced by these words, *"Let us make man in Our image, and let him rule . . . over all the Earth"* (Genesis 1:27). Man was created to join God as a "junior co-ruler" of the Earth.

There is a fascinating verse in Psalm 8 that is so bold that the translators in earlier days gave it a safer translation, because they couldn't believe what it was saying! In the Hebrew language David wrote this in Psalm 8:5 regarding God's creation of Man: *"You have made him a little less than Elohim (God), and crowned him with glory and honor."*

This statement is so incredible that the early translators substituted *"angels"* for *"Elohim."* They were uncomfortable in their false humility to ever think that David was saying that Adam, being created in the image of God (Genesis 1:27), was so high in the rank and order of all creation that he lacked but little of God. Yet, that is what David wrote.

Before sin came into the Garden, Adam fully reflected the awesomeness of being patterned after God. Adam was endowed with all the gifts he needed for ruling, and then was made a co-superintendent of the Earth with God Himself. Imagine this: God created the heavens and the Earth in six days, and when He rested on the seventh day, it's as if He slapped the dust off His hands, looked at Adam and said, "Ok, your turn; let's see what you can create."

We can see the power and authority of Adam's rank in the world with his first assignment. Adam was given the charge to name the animals.

How were those animals created? God *spoke* them into existence.

How were those animals named? Adam *spoke* the names into existence. Adam demonstrated his dominion and authority over the animal kingdom by creating and speaking their names. This demonstrates that Adam belonged to the same class of creative, speaking, and ruling beings as God.

Psalm 8 was no exaggeration!

However, when sin came, man lost the power and authority that went with his original co-regency. In the Garden, the Tree of Life that represented the presence of God's life was cordoned off from man. "God's Life" was no longer available. In fact, that Life was no longer offered on planet Earth until a baby was born in a manger, and John declared, "In Him was life, and the life was the light of men" (John 1:4). Therefore, when you and Christ became one spirit with each other (1 Corinthians 6:17), that original life from the Tree of Life becomes yours, in your spirit. The power and authority of God's life returned to earth in Jesus Christ, and that power and authority is given to his followers, when they receive Him.

When He was on the Earth, one of the ways that Christ exercised His kingly power and authority was to use words. We manifest His power and authority in the same way: we use words. With our words we can rule over the conflicts in our mind and emotions. We can take authority over the shame of our story, and over the demonic, and demonstrate that we belong to the same class of creative, speaking, ruling beings as God.

Paul tells us some of his personal story in 2 Corinthians, and how he uses words to reign in life. In 4:8 he describes the difficulty of being a traveling missionary and struggling with personal conflicts. He names four conditions that he encounters, and they are quite familiar to us today. These four conditions are the kind that can "trigger" the shame of our backstory, and move us to walk in our false self and our fleshly stronghold-ways. That is, these four conditions trigger our posing and posturing, and our anger and controlling, our yelling and manipulating of others, our fussing, fighting, quarreling, withdrawing, hating, judging, and more.

Here's what Paul says in 2 Corinthians 4:8-9: *"We are afflicted in every way, but not crushed; perplexed, but not despairing; persecuted, but not forsaken; struck down, but not destroyed."*

Paul says that he got afflicted. But he did not end up crushed. He got perplexed, but he did not end up in in despair. He was persecuted, but he didn't run around like a victim crying that God had forsaken him. Fourth, Paul says that he got knocked down. But it did not destroy him.

He didn't live in victimhood and passivity.

But consider the life of most Christians. We have hurtful memories from our childhood that gave birth to destructive lies in our minds, and those lies gave birth to toxic emotions. Now as an adult, in our marriages, our families, and at the work place, new events happen that trigger these old lies and old emotions. In my life, I go through experiences that create the same difficulties that Paul mentions, and it's easy for me to get into the victim mind-set. I get afflicted, perplexed, persecuted, and knocked down by insults, accusations, labels, rejections, and betrayals, and I become demoralized and confused. It stirs up the same old lies and toxic emotions from my childhood, and it's easy to cry out that I am once again crushed, squeezed, or treated unfairly. I can end up feeling hemmed in, jammed up, defeated, and despairing, depressed and moping, running around whining that God doesn't love me, or He's forgotten me, perhaps He's punishing me, left me behind and abandoned me. It's enough to send me into a spiritual downward ruin.

I've seen it ruin people so badly spiritually that they take a vacation from the faith for a few years.

This happens to all of us.

But wait!

Did you notice? It didn't happen to Paul.[10]

He says that he *did not* get crushed; he *did not* get depressed; he *did not* whine about God abandoning him; he *did not* get spiritually ruined. Different from our responses, Paul did not become a victim. He walked in triumph.

How did he do it?

What did Paul do that we are not doing?

He spoke! He opened his mouth and took authority over his conflicts: "*What I believe, I speak . . .*" (2 Corinthians 4:13b).

Whatever Paul believes from Scripture about the love and protection of God, those verses are His source of

---

[10] In 2 Corinthians 1:8-9, Paul does reveal that he once was in such despair that he was crushed to the point of thinking he might die. Obviously, he had a healing recovery with God, and learned God's power is made perfect in weakness (12:9), thus, he can speak what he does in 4:8-9.

strength and comfort. He spoke the Scripture. He spoke what he believed. His spiritual conquest was built on the power and authority of being a member of the same class of creative, speaking, ruling beings as God. In fact, he says he got the idea *to speak Scripture* from reading one of the psalms (verse 13a). By faith, Paul spoke what he believed, and spoke it when he got afflicted, perplexed, persecuted, or knocked down. He knew that God was using the conflict to make him more godly, to bring death to his flesh and to reveal more of the resurrection life of Christ (vv. 10-11).

Whatever happens to us in life today, we don't have to keep living our same old story. We can overcome it by running off at the mouth. We can have a more triumphant attitude of faith today, like Paul, if we will open our mouth and start speaking what we believe to be true in Scripture. When Jesus was afflicted with temptation in the wilderness, He spoke the Word of God and the enemy left.

He didn't just *believe* the Word of God. He *spoke* it.

Beyond being identified in Righteousness, Paul spoke his righteousness.

When you are afflicted, don't get crushed. Change the direction of the story like Paul and quote Scripture. Speak what you believe: *"I am one spirit with Christ!"* (1 Corinthians 6:17).

"I have received the abundance of grace and the gift of righteousness, and I will reign with Christ," (Romans 5:17b).

"In all things I am more than a conqueror through Him who loves me . . . for nothing present . . . nor any thing to come . . . no power . . . can separate me from the love of God in Christ Jesus my Lord," (Romans 8:37-39).

When you are perplexed and don't understand what is happening with you or around you, or if you wonder where God is, you can reign over that emerging story and cancel it. You can speak what you believe:

"I can know the things of God . . . for I have the mind of Christ," (1 Corinthians 2:12,16).

The Spirit of Truth abides in me . . . and He will guide me into truth," (John 14:26; 16:33).

"I do not worship a God of confusion, but a God of peace . . . and He is my wisdom . . ." (1 Corinthians 14:33; 1 Corinthians 1:30).

When you are persecuted, whether it is by the world because you are standing in righteousness, or if it is from your own foolishness, you should always know that God is walking in it with you, and He is still a good God with no condemnation for you. You can speak verses like this:

I am blessed to be persecuted because the Kingdom of Heaven is mine, . . . and my reward is going to be great" (Matthew 5:10,12).

*"I will give thanks to the Lord, for He is good . . .
He sends me His word and heals me, and delivers
me from destruction,"* (Psalm 107:1,20).

*"The Lord redeems the life of His servants; none of
those who take refuge in Him will be condemned . . .
There is no condemnation to those who are in Christ
Jesus,"* (Psalm 34:22; Romans 8:1).

If you are devastated by horribly bad news, if you are
"slugged in the gut" by a death or loss, by adultery in your
marriage, by your spouse walking out, or by your personal
dreams being shattered; if you are knocked down emotionally or spiritually, you can still quote Scripture:

*"The Lord is near to me, the brokenhearted, and He
saves my crushed spirit. Many are the afflictions of
the righteous, but the Lord delivers me out of them
all,"* (Psalm 34:18, 19).

*"My steps are established by the Lord, and I delight
in His way, and though I fall, I will not fall on my
head, for the Lord is holding my hand,"* (Psalm
37:23,24).

*"Though the righteous man falls seven times, I will
get up again!"* (Proverbs 24:16).

Be the creative, speaking, ruling being that you are. You
are a holy, righteous child of God who is going through a
rough patch. Don't let your backstory repeat itself. Don't

let the schemes of the enemy take control of you. You take control of your story by walking in the power and authority of the Holy Spirit and speaking God's Word!

We worship a God who calls into being that which does not exist (Romans 4:17). Let's join with Him as creative, speaking, ruling beings made in His image, and call into being what does not exist. Let's call into existence the faith, peace, hope, and perseverance of Christ in our situations. Let's rule over our old stories and any new chapters the enemy has planned for us. You are a holy, righteous child of God who was once abused, neglected, abandoned, rejected, or betrayed—but your past story does not have to rule your present. After your healing prayers (Chapters 15 and 16), get up and speak your healing. Speak the truth Christ spoke over you in the healing prayers. Read Scripture and find more verses that speak to the issues of your story, and speak them. Read them, receive them, believe them, and speak them!

Jesus said, "My words are spirit and life," (John 6:63). During His ministry on earth, when Jesus spoke, the Holy Spirit anointed His words to make them life-giving. His words were filled with the Holy Spirit, making Christ a life-giving Spirit (1 Corinthians 15:45). People were made right with God through the words of Jesus. People got healed of diseases at His words. Storms dissipated when Jesus spoke. Demons took flight when Jesus commanded. His words were filled with the life of God!

In Mark 11:22-23, Jesus told us that if we had such faith from God then we could speak to mountains and command them to be taken up and thrown into the sea. *Speak* to the mountain. Jesus did not tell us to pray to the Father about the mountain. He did not tell us to talk to our pastor about the mountain. He told us to open our mouths and command! Don't beg. Don't plead. Speak to the mountain and tell it to go!

> **You have in your life what you speak with your mouth.**

David *spoke* to Goliath. He told that man-mountain that he was going to cut off his head, and it happened just as *he said*! David knew from Scripture that the Lord of Hosts was the God of the Israeli army, that the battle is the Lord's, and He "will give you into our hands!" The nation of Israel knew that God "will curse those who curse you" (Genesis 12:3), but only David believed it. Then he spoke it! David spoke the Word of God over the situation, and he had in his life what he spoke with his mouth. Goliath died that day as David said he would.

Kings don't beg or plead; they command and decree!

We are kings. We are members of the same class of creative, speaking, ruling beings as David. Take authority. Use your mouth! Reign in life by speaking what you believe.

CHAPTER 22

Pray for A Breakthrough

"Lord, I'm willing to be made willing; to be delivered from myself."

A major thesis of this book has been to claim that something is missing in our discipleship training. We are failing to deal adequately with the "interior condition" of the disciple. We are not helping believers make a dynamic change at the level of identity.

What I have proposed is a healing process that could be called Identity-Based Transformation. The process is summarized here:

Life is painful, and it has a damaging effect on the soul. After becoming a Christian, it is the interior condition of the soul that can be the greatest hindrance to Christian growth. Healing and delivering the soul from the pain, anger, fear, and loneliness is so necessary if the discipleship process is to be more full and complete.

These hurtful emotions in the soul come with silent messages of shame. We begin to hate some things about ourselves, or we hate how God has made us, and we build an identity around this shame. This is our Shame-based identity, and it develops inside our soul. As we perceive ourselves in shame, so it becomes our identity (Proverbs 23:7).

Because this identity is itself adding more pain to the soul, we develop our own strategy for coping and managing our lives. The coping behaviors we develop for surviving become known in the New Testament as *the flesh: all the ways apart from God that we seek to get our needs met; to protect ourselves and to provide for ourselves.*

The flesh doesn't seek out healing. The flesh is more about hiding. Since we don't know how to heal the shame, we develop a "False Self" as a front to hide the shame. We create a "super-self" and send him to church and work; a false self who can perform "our best life now!" routine. This way, hopefully, no one could imagine that we have such shame hidden in our hearts.

We hide our Shame-Based Identity by living in the phoniness of our False Self, which sabotages any attempt to grow spiritually. At least, until "Jesus comes with grace and truth" (John 1:14). After our initial salvation experience, Truth is like feedback from God. Through reading Scripture, through sermons, through meaningful conversations with friends, and especially through broken, painful relationships, Truth comes to reveal our story of brokenness. Then grace is there to heal our story, memory by memory. Truth comes to reveal to us the pain in our heart, the wounds in our soul, the abuse in our heart, and the lies in our head. Then Grace heals us wound by wound, prayer by prayer.

This is how we deal with the interior condition of our heart. Memory by memory, prayer by prayer, we bring the pain, anger, fear, and loneliness into the presence of God. We let Grace lead us into dialogue with Him, Who gives us truth, feedback, and further epiphanies. He diminishes our shame, as we renounce the lies and receive His healing words.

This is the way of changing at the level of identity. It is story work. During this transformational prayer work, the Shame-based identity falls away, as our true identity in Christ emerges. Spiritual growth, if it is to be lasting and significant, must be made at the level of Identity. But Identity-based transformation requires a breakthrough.

Are you ready for a breakthrough? Are you sick of yourself, yet? Are your loved ones ready for your breakthrough? Here's how mine started.

The Lord of the Breakthrough

Before I stood before my church and resigned as their pastor for my sexual sin, I confessed it days earlier to my board of elders. They immediately placed me on a sabbatical leave from my duties, a leave that lasted for about six weeks before I returned to read my resignation to the congregation. During those first few weeks, though, I left town.

It was on one particular Sunday morning, an hour's drive away from home, while visiting (hiding out!) at another church, that God first broke through my shell of self-protection and the fear of my story. On this morning I began my healing process.

As if he had flipped a switch in my heart, I immediately burst into tears; sobbed and sobbed; and cried uncontrollably non-stop for fifteen to twenty minutes! Friends gathered around me, taken by surprise at my uncontrollable sobbing. Thankfully, it happened after the sermon. The service was over and the auditorium was thinning out when Griff walked down the row behind me, and stopped. He put his hands on my shoulders in a gesture of affection, and immediately at his touch the dam of tears broke. I had not dared to say a word about my situation, but now my friends realized that this sabbatical leave from my church obviously meant that I was in some kind of spiritual trouble.

Several minutes of gut-wrenching sobbing will make a man limp and wobbly, so a couple of friends literally had to hold me up and help me walk out to the car. In the car Rose looked at me caringly and said, "Pray for a breakthrough, Carter . . . in Isaiah 28 the prophet spoke about David's battle with the Philistines at Mount Perazim, the 'mountain of the breakthrough,' where God delivered David from his enemies. Pray for a breakthrough."

Rose had no idea what was happening in my life. She knew nothing of my secret addiction. No one knew . . . yet. But she could hear from the Holy Spirit, and I knew that this was His word for me.

Pray for a breakthrough. I am the Lord of the Breakthrough.

So, I went home and looked up Isaiah 28, and this passage of Scripture was my bread for the next several weeks. I read through it daily. I didn't like what I read, at first. A breakthrough starts off sounding quite scary.

Therefore, hear the word of the LORD, of scoffers, . . . Because you have said, "We have made a covenant with death; with Sheol we have made a pact. The overwhelming scourge will not reach us when it passes by; for we have made Falsehood our refuge and we have concealed ourselves with our Deception," (Isaiah 28:14-15 NASB).

Notice that Yahweh, the personal and covenant-keeping God, is speaking to His own people and He calls them scoffers. From the book of Proverbs we can discover that those who are called scoffers are people who are struggling with a hardness of heart. They have a sinful flesh pattern that they stubbornly hang onto. They do not want to give it up, for it serves well to protect them, to provide for them, to promote them, or it pleasures them.

Worse, they are haughty in their arrogance and self-certainty (the False-Self). What is it they are so certain about? They are arrogant about their hiding place. These people *think* they are getting away with their sins. They *think* they will not receive the scourge of discipline from the

Lord God; therefore, they think that their arrogance and lies are a refuge from God.

When we choose never to deal with compulsive, controlling sin in our lives, then we make a covenant with death. To agree with this flesh pattern, and to never confront it, is to make an agreement with falsehood, and hide behind the deception, only to bring spiritual death (ruin) to ourselves and others with our secret sin. Over time a hardness of heart sets in, an ironic sense of arrogance emerges, and we develop a false sense of security that the lies we continue to tell ourselves are working! All the while we are walking into spiritual ruin, for sin brings death.

What has happened to us when we become so hardened by our sin that our loyalty to that sin is likened to a covenant? The world calls it addiction. The Bible calls it slavery. The world says it's a disease. The Bible says it's wretchedness (Romans 7:24).

In my addiction I had lost the ability to be scandalized by my own sin. My devotion to my addiction had the strength of a covenant, and even I believed my lies. Long earlier I had lost the fear of being scourged by God's loving discipline. I was losing my passion. I was losing my heart. My sermons were banal, and I foolishly thought that I was well hidden behind my secrets. In this condition, there was no way that I could be delivered or healed. The only way out was for God to break through this *covenant with death*.

Remember in John 5, when Jesus came to the Pool of Bethesda, where He met someone who apparently had a covenant with death, too? Ancient manuscripts reveal that the reason people hung out at this pool was because of a religious superstition that angels from heaven would occasionally stir the water with their wings, heralding through the ripples that there was power for healing to the first person to get into the water. I can make up in my mind that Jesus knew of this tradition, and was not only perturbed with the people of Israel for believing it, but also with the spiritual leaders for allowing this magic-doctrine to be perpetuated.

Now, beyond his physical incapacitation, there was something else wrong with this man by the pool, something which Jesus called sin (v. 14). This sin was not identified, but it might have been the case that this invalid had found comfort in his covenant with death, comfort in being well content to be a victim. One Bible commentator's research discovered the same revelation made recently on a television news show, that even in ancient times a beggar often made a good living by playing the role of a victim. Perhaps, then, it was in a spirit of frustration that Jesus approached the man (a beggar-victim?) beside the pool and asked, "Do you want to get well?" (v. 6).

I used to think that was such a strange question. Of course the man wanted to get well. Everyone wants to get well! Yet, in the first few weeks and months of my own recovery, when I desperately wanted to run from recovery and run back to the comfort of being a victim—after I had nearly lost my family, had resigned my pastorate, was humiliated in front of my church, and publicly embarrassed—after all that, I still wanted to *act out in my foolish behavior!* It was then, early one Friday morning, when the Holy Spirit brought this question of Jesus into my mind. The Lord Jesus personally asked me, too, "Do you want to get well?"

That Friday morning I saw the power of the question. What a great question it is for someone who has made a covenant with death. For I heard my own answer emerge from my soul. Amazingly, my answer was, "No. I don't want to get well. I love my addiction . . . we've grown up together . . . I need it . . . it has comforted me, and I can't say goodbye."

Oh, my, I realized. *I didn't want to get well.*

I couldn't believe what I'd heard in my soul. In the midst of my own struggle to break the addiction, in these early months of emotional agony, in the throes of my own enormous pain, I didn't want to say goodbye to my addiction!

No one will ever break a stronghold in this life without the *desire* to be free. As James wrote, you cannot be double-minded and expect to find freedom (James 1:8). If part of my mind joyfully concurs with the law of God (Romans 7:22), but another part of my mind happily loves being under the control of the stronghold, then I am a man with a divided soul. I cannot get well. Into this condition there must come a gracious breakthrough by the Lord Jesus Christ.

I obviously could not get a breakthrough on my own, not with a covenant-like agreement with sin and deception. If I had the capacity for breakthrough within me, then I would have given it to myself. Since I didn't have it within me, it must come from outside of myself. It must come from God and others that He will use in my life.

Breakthrough work is alien to our normal attempts at Christian growth. But when we are in the throes of our own stubborn commitment to a sin that has grown as a defense to the pain of our story, then we need an alien work. We need an extraordinary work of God in our lives, and this is how our Isaiah 28 passage concludes:

For the Lord will rise up as on Mount Perazim; as in the Valley of Gibeon, He will be roused; to do his deed—strange is His deed! and to work His work— alien is his work! (Isaiah 28:21)

The New American Standard translates it, "His unusual, extraordinary work!" It is a painful work when God breaks through the arrogance of our lies of self-protection, where we are hiding as a victim to our story, claiming we are too crippled to live any other way. For God to deliver us from these strongholds of our mind, it will feel strange and alien. It is not the normal work of our show-up-and-applaud version of Christianity. Breakthrough work is scary at first, but comes to be so blessed as the work progresses. I felt like I had been betrayed by those that loved me, as I gave myself to this alien form of discipline. But as I yielded to grace and truth, I saw my story in the fullness of my pain, my lies, and my hiding and posing. Slowly but deliberately, God lead me into the healing of my story, the healing of my soul, and the triumph of my spirit-man over my story.

Pray for a breakthrough, for this is when you will learn about a greater grace (James 4:6), a grace that supersedes your first draw of grace when you were born-again. A greater grace is also what this book is about, learning something about Grace that most people never learn without a deep spiritual journey. I hope you have a breakthrough in healing and deliverance from the wounds, the sin-patterns, the Shame-Based Identity and the False Self—and all that is keeping you from the love of the Father, the grace of the Lord Jesus, and the companionship of the Holy Spirit. Pray for a breakthrough into His intimacy.

Prayer for a Breakthrough

Dear Heavenly Father,

I know that Your desire is for me to know You and the power of the Resurrection, but I fear the suffering and the journey to the cross to be conformed to your death (Phil 3:10).

I need to be delivered from myself; I need a breakthrough.

I'm willing to be made willing; to let this stronghold be broken; that You might do whatever it takes to set me free.

Grant me a sorrow that leads to repentance (2 Corinthians 7:10); lead me to someone in the Body of Christ with whom I can trust this issue; lead me to someone who can help me break strongholds and walk into freedom.

In Jesus' Name.

Are you interested in
PURE HEART WEEKEND?
Contact Carter about scheduling one in your church.
carter@carterfeatherston.com

As I wrote in the beginning of this book, our discipleship programs are not targeting our interior condition: we are neglecting the personal history of emotional hurt and brokenness, and the diminished sense of identity. **Pure Heart Weekend** is about helping people discover this blind spot—their shame-based identity out of which they operate, and then help them experience the healing of pain, the freedom from shame, and the power of their new identity in Christ. Let Carter come lead your small group in an encounter with God through his teaching, life-mapping, and healing prayer. It is a life-changing weekend.

> *I no longer have a "heaviness of spirit." I no longer have the horrible dreams of my past life. Because of Pure Heart, I experienced a true identity change. I am living in my freedom in Christ. I thank God every day that I attended a Pure Heart Weekend. It has changed my life.*
> —Christie, Las Vegas

> *After my wife and I went through Pure Heart, the conversations we had were <u>amazing</u>! We spoke about things that I never even knew we weren't speaking about! We're also praying together more. Christ is reigning in our house now, and even our kids see the difference in us. They humorously speak of our parenting in terms of "before Pure Heart Weekend, and after Pure Heart Weekend."*
> —Kevin, Las Vegas

> *Before the weekend I carried a ton of shame and felt emotionally paralyzed at times. Pure Heart Weekend provided a safe and loving environment to be vulnerable and real with a painful past. I experienced a healing of my heart that was nothing short of a miracle and learned tools to continue on living in the identity and freedom that Christ always intended for me.*
> —Gracie, Chicago

> *I did not know what to expect when I came to Pure Heart Wknd, but God shocked me. Stunned me! He stepped into that weekend in a way I've never knew He could. Old wounds were healed, and it changed my life dramatically.*
> —Tammy, Hammond, LA

> *Being a local church pastor nothing is more frustrating than not being able to help people. After I went through Pure Heart Weekend I knew I could never lead church the same way. Over the past year we have taken small groups of people in our church through Pure Heart Weekend, helping them experience the healing grace of Jesus in ways a sermon doesn't always do. As a pastor, I cannot recommend it more highly.*
> —Marty Williams, Pastor of
> Anthem Community Church, Henderson, NV

BIO

Carter Featherston, Th.M.

Restore One Ministries

Website: http://www.carterfeatherston.com

Carter Featherston is a pastoral-counselor, retreat leader and speaker. He leads a retreat for spiritual transformation called Pure Heart Weekend, through which he has helped hundreds of people change at the level of identity through life mapping, healing prayer and breaking strongholds. Carter is also the author of the eBook, *God Knows Your Struggle; and He Wants to Help* (Amazon), a book on breaking the control of sexual strongholds and shame. He and his wife, Cindy, have three adult children and two grandchildren. He and Cindy live in Covington, LA with their two dogs, Sami and Zoey.